The Flawed Family of God

The Flawed Family of God

Stories about the Imperfect Families of Genesis

Carolyn B. Helsel

Song-Mi Suzie Park

WJK WESTMINSTER
JOHN KNOX PRESS
LOUISVILLE · KENTUCKY

First edition
Published by Westminster John Knox Press
Louisville, Kentucky

21 22 23 24 25 26 27 28 29 30—10 9 8 7 6 5 4 3 2 1

Unless otherwise indicated, Scripture quotations are from the New Revised Standard Version of the Bible, copyright © 1989 by the Division of Christian Education of the National Council of the Churches of Christ in the U.S.A., and are used by permission.

Book design by Sharon Adams
Cover design by Barbara LeVan Fisher, www.levanfisherdesign.com
Cover illustration: Turkana Afternoon, 1994 *(oil on canvas)* © *Tilly Willis / Bridgeman Images*

Library of Congress Cataloging-in-Publication Data

Names: Helsel, Carolyn B., author. | Park, Song-Mi Suzie, author.
Title: The flawed family of God : stories about the imperfect families of
  Genesis / Carolyn B. Helsel, Song-Mi Suzie Park.
Description: First edition. | Louisville, Kentucky : Westminster John Knox
  Press, 2021. | Summary: "This Bible study examines the families of
  Genesis, starting with how the Adam and Eve story encompasses far more
  ways of being family-including singleness-than most of us think, and
  shows us that the ups and downs of the relationship between Abraham,
  Sarah, Hagar, and Ishmael can help us understand the complicated dynamic
  of blended families"-- Provided by publisher.
Identifiers: LCCN 2020047404 (print) | LCCN 2020047405 (ebook) | ISBN
  9780664265984 (paperback) | ISBN 9781646980383 (ebook)
Subjects: LCSH: Bible. Genesis--Criticism, interpretation, etc. |
  Families--Biblical teaching.
Classification: LCC BS1238.F34 H45 2021 (print) | LCC BS1238.F34 (ebook)
  | DDC 222.11/30685--dc23
LC record available at https://lccn.loc.gov/2020047404
LC ebook record available at https://lccn.loc.gov/2020047405

Most Westminster John Knox Press books are available at special quantity discounts when purchased in bulk by corporations, organizations, and special-interest groups. For more information, please e-mail SpecialSales@wjkbooks.com.

Contents

Acknowledgments

To write a book about flawed families seems almost a confession, because you cannot write about what you do not know, right? And to some extent, that is true in my life: I grew up in a beautifully flawed family with four sisters and a younger brother, with plenty of family drama over the years. Throughout my childhood, we attended a large church downtown in the city where we lived, and everyone going to church always seemed so perfect. Dressed in perfect clothes, looking like their lives were in perfect order, with cheerful expressions on everyone's faces showing they were the emblems of success. I felt my family was the only one with problems. What a relief it was to read the Bible and find out that was certainly not the case!

So let me first begin by thanking my wonderful family: my parents and each of my siblings, for the support you all have provided me and one another over the years, and for your faithfulness amidst the many ups and downs we have known together. To my mom and dad, thank you for taking us all to church so that we could hear the Scriptures read and proclaimed, and I could learn from these texts how flawed families were not only part of God's greater story but they played a starring role! I continue to experience God's grace and love through you all. Thank you.

To my husband, Phil, who has made the creation of our own family such a joyful journey, I cannot thank you enough. For our children who daily teach me how to wonder at the world, I am so grateful. My sweet family offers me the opportunity to see God at work in birding, poetry, painting, story-writing, and backyard chickens.

I also am so glad I got invited by Suzie Park to work on this book with her. It was her idea to cowrite this book, and I have learned so much along the way from her brilliant scholarship. Suzie, thank you for trusting me enough to invite me into the journey of writing together! I was amazed at how seamlessly we worked on this project, and how fun it was to write.

Finally, I have to say a huge thank-you to the dear friends who shared their stories with me so that I could share them here. Kyle Walker and his husband, Nelis Potgieter, in chapter 4, Jen Hunt in chapter 5, Margaret Aymer in chapter 6, and Susan Cottrell in chapter 7. All of them were so gracious to give of their time and to tell their stories of witness: while the biblical stories so often provide *bad* examples for how to live as a family, these modern-day people of faith are setting better examples for us to follow, and to all of them I say a loud and deep thank-you!

For all the families out there who need to hear that their struggle is real, that God is with us when we are not at our best, and that there are people navigating family life in better ways than we may have imagined in the past, this book is for you.

CAROLYN HELSEL

Many people were helpful to the conception, writing, and completion of this work. First, I want to thank the members of the Moveable Feast pastor cohort, who asked me to participate in their meeting as a scholar in 2018. The idea for this book came from overhearing members of this cohort talking about the lack of resources for thematic preaching. Thank you for graciously letting me participate and also for letting me listen in on your conversations.

Though the initial idea stemmed from the cohort, it was primarily my coauthor, Carolyn Helsel, who offered the motivation and gentle push needed to complete this work. Without her, I most certainly would have taken a bit too long. I am thankful for her energy and am grateful to be her colleague and coauthor.

Carolyn is one of many wonderful people I get to work with at Austin Presbyterian Theological Seminary, all of whom are kind, thoughtful, interesting, and fun.

I am also grateful to Stephen Milburn and Julia Burkley, my research aides, as well as Robert Ratcliff and other editors at Westminster John Knox for their help in improving this work.

Attendees and fellow presenters at the Bible and Practical Theology section of the 2019 AAR/SBL meeting asked wise questions and provided great feedback when Carolyn and I presented on this book.

Thanks also to Kevin Lam, who faithfully and carefully read, edited, and offered suggestions. He has surely made this work better.

Finally, to my mother and father, who instilled in me a love of the stories in the Bible, thank you.

Suzie Park

Introduction

"Biblical" Families?

What does the Bible say about what it means to be a family? And what does the Bible have to do with the current struggles of families today?

A husband and wife are worried about their sons who keep bullying, fighting, and teasing each other, so much so that the parents worry about their sons' physical safety. Their fighting has caused a split in the family as each parent lines up to the side of one child or the other.

An older couple have been trying for years to conceive a child without success. They have given up hope of being able to have their own child, so they go through a process of surrogacy. Another woman carries the child for them. But then the unexpected happens: the surrogate wants to keep the child she has borne, and the couple struggling with infertility conceive a child of their own. What happens now to the child conceived through surrogacy and to the woman who carried that child for the couple?

A man feels called to leave his hometown and travel to a new country with promising new opportunities ahead. The wife feels she has no say in the matter. How will their marriage weather the relocation?

With a bit of creative imagination, perhaps you have picked up on the fact that the previous three vignettes were from the Bible: Genesis 25, Genesis 16 and 17, and Genesis 12. But with that same creativity, perhaps you could hear the similarities to what contemporary families are experiencing: fears about bullies, dealing with infertility and blended families, and family moves.

As you read this book we hope you understand that the stories of the Bible, particularly the stories about families, have relevance for the

1

experiences of families today. What do we mean by "relevance"? We mean that they relate to our experiences in that these stories tell us something about what it means to be a family, including the struggles inherent to family life.

How We Read the Bible

When we say these stories have relevance, we also mean that they are important. These stories are important because they are part of the biblical canon, the books that have been passed on from generation to generation through religious faith communities that have viewed these texts as special and authoritative in some way. For hundreds of years before the birth of Jesus, Jewish communities of faith would tell and hear, and eventually write down and collect, these stories about the patriarchs and matriarchs of the Hebrew people. As Christians began forming new faith communities following the ministry of Jesus, they too adopted these Scriptures as their own, reading the stories of Genesis along with the rest of the books we call the "Old Testament," or more appropriately, the "Hebrew Bible," side by side with what we term the "New Testament."

For hundreds of years, these stories were read only by learned priests and scribes, but they were shared with other believers through storytelling and preaching at the synagogues. The purpose of such storytelling was to remind people of faith that God accompanies us through life, including the ups and downs and moments of discouragement and suffering. The stories of our faith continue to serve this purpose, reminding us that God sees our suffering and pain and that God promises to be with us throughout our lives.

The ways we read the Bible are as different as the people who read the Bible, but there are some general commonalities across different groups. One way to read the Bible is as literature: seeing the Bible as a group of stories compiled thousands of years ago, much like the stories of Homer's *Iliad* or *Odyssey*. Because these are stories written in another time period and for another culture, they may not feel directly relevant to our daily lives since they do not connect to our religious communities.

Another way of reading the Bible is devotionally. This way looks to the Bible as a book with pages full of messages directly from God. When people speak of the Bible as God's Word, sometimes they mean specifically that the Bible was actually dictated by God to each author who participated in writing it down. For people who read the Bible this way, they are reading the stories in Genesis as a direct message from God, which may include that all of the events in the stories took place exactly as they were written: the six days of creation, the order of which life forms existed first, and so on. For people who read the Bible this way, the stories in Genesis can seem like a prescription for how life *ought* to be lived.

But there is another way of reading the Bible, and this way can also be devotional; but to distinguish it from the paragraph above, let us use a different term: *relationally*. Reading the Bible "relationally" means that we are in a relationship with the Bible. The God described in its pages reflects and is intertwined in complex ways with the God we know from personal experience and from the communities of faith who have surrounded us since our birth. We are in a relationship with these stories because they have been told to us from our youngest memories by people of our faith communities or traditions who also believe that God is reflected in and through the stories in the Bible.

To read the Bible, and in particular, the book of Genesis, *relationally* means that we believe God speaks to us through these stories, though not necessarily in ways that we assume. Just as God was in relationship with the people whose stories we learn about in Genesis, so too God is still in relationship with us today. It is important to realize that reading the Bible this way means that we see the Bible as *not the same as God*. God is *not* the Bible. Some people want to read the Bible as if the Bible were God, and we see that as idolatry. The Bible is not God. And yet the Bible is one of the best sources we have for coming to an understanding of God and how communities of faith have understood God working in their lives for ages. To read the Bible *relationally* means that we are in a relationship with the Bible, and that relationship is separate from the relationship we have with God.

To take this to another level: in order to have a relationship with God or to have a good relationship with the Bible, you do not need to believe that God created the world in six days. You do not need to believe the story of creation in Genesis 1–3 is a historical and scientific description in order to have a relationship with the God who created all of the expansive and ever-expanding universe as we know it, and you do not need to place unfair expectations on the Bible to be something it is not. You can still have a relationship with the Bible, learning from it and letting it teach you about who God is, without expecting it to teach you about geology or biology.

Reading the Bible Relationally
and Learning about Biblical Families

So what does how we read the Bible have to do with the families portrayed by the Bible? A lot, it turns out. If we read the Bible as only the absolute words from God's mouth, we may tend to see the descriptions of biblical families as somehow reflective of the way God intended for families to be. That is, we may misinterpret the biblical text as a kind of easy do-it-yourself instructional manual. But there is a lot of pain and abuse and inappropriate ways of relating to one another in these stories. If we took these words as absolutely the way God intended life to be—as prescriptive—we may believe that God wants us to suffer, and we may unintentionally harm others by suggesting their suffering is willed by God. Especially when we are talking about children, it is essential that we reject any notion that God wants them to suffer abuse from their parents or from others.

But reading the Bible *relationally* means that we can talk back to some of these texts. We can get angry at them, and we can ask questions about them. We can get angry at the God or the various characters mentioned in these stories who allowed these things to happen. As we see in the book of Psalms, God's people are constantly expressing their anger at God when things go wrong. We can continue to do the same today *because we are in relationship with God, and we are in a relationship with the Bible.* We can get mad at how Adam blames Eve for the Fall. We can get mad at the way Abram treats his wife Sarai when he passes her off as his sister to the pharaoh in Egypt. We can get mad at the story in Genesis 22 where God supposedly tells Abraham to sacrifice (kill) his son Isaac. We can get mad at the story in Genesis 34 that we never heard about as children: the rape of Dinah. We can be in a relationship with God and question why God would allow this and many other stories of abuse and torture to remain in the Bible.

To read the Bible relationally means that we can come back to it, even when we have not been immersed in its pages for many years, having turned our backs on its painful messages. The God who has met us there in the Bible's pages is still there with us today, and God will meet us again in these stories. And that may be exactly why you need to return to it: pain in your own family or the situations your family is facing may be making you wonder where God is. Rather than finding picture-perfect families in the Bible, we find mirrors of our own dysfunctional dynamics. And in those family portraits that the Bible presents us with, we see ourselves and the experiences of our loved ones, perhaps in new ways. And just as God was with those families, so too is God with us now, seeing us in our pain and struggles and wanting us to know God accompanies us.

God accompanies the families of the Bible, and God uses them and works through them in often surprising ways. As we look at these stories together, we hope that you will experience God accompanying you as well.

Outline of the Book

We center our relational reading of families in the Bible by focusing on the stories in the book of Genesis. Genesis is not only filled with stories about the first human families, but as the first book of the Bible, it also colors how we think about families both in the Bible and in our own lives. As such, each chapter of this book will take a careful look at one particular story in Genesis that concerns an issue faced by a family. For each story, we will first examine the biblical tale in detail, pointing out interesting and important features, and also explaining how the story might differ from the way it is usually remembered or taught in churches. This close reading of the biblical story is followed by a discussion of the modern relevance of the tale—that is, the ways in which the biblical story affects and is related to similar issues or instances in our lives today.

To offer a brief overview of the various stories and issues we will consider in this work, we begin our exploration of families in chapter 1 by showing how the two myths about the creation of humanity in Genesis 1–3 serve as a blueprint for a diverse reimagining of families. Continuing the saga begun by the creation myths, chapter 2 focuses on the tragedy of Cain and Abel (Gen. 4:1–16) by looking at the impact of competition, rivalry, and jealousy in families. Our study of dysfunctions in the family continues in chapter 3 as we consider the lingering effects of trauma on Noah and his family in Genesis 6:5–9:28.

We delve into issues related to family moves and trailing spouses in chapter 4 by examining Abram and Sarai's migration in Genesis 12:1–20; and in chapter 5, we focus on Sarai's infertility—a problem experienced by many biblical characters—and one which still affects people today. The issue of infertility leads to discussion in chapter 6 about the challenges faced by blended families, such as those created by remarriage or adoption, as we explore the first blended family in the Hebrew Bible: Abraham, Sarah, Hagar, and Ishmael.

Chapter 7 turns to the weighty issue of child abuse and other instances of child "sacrifice" in the family, including the difficulties of someone coming out as LBGTQ, by examining the near sacrifice of Isaac by his father in Genesis 22. Speaking of family problems, competition among parents is the focus of our discussion in chapter 8, which considers the troubling situation of Rachel and Leah, sisters who are both married to Jacob. Chapter 9 examines the long, complex story of the twins Jacob and Esau, as they move from trauma, familial wounds, and estrangement to reunion and reconciliation. And finally, chapter 10 looks at the irreplaceable nature of a family member as we discuss how a death affects the family unit.

Hopes for This Book

Our exploration of these family stories and issues is centered on three goals. The first is that you will be able to see the relevance and connections between these biblical texts and the struggles of families today. This means looking deeper at the book of Genesis and exploring stories that may have been missed in the traditional Sunday school curriculum you learned as a child.

For instance, the story of Noah and the ark is not only told to children in Sunday school, but it is also one of the most widely recognized pictures for decorating the rooms in which we teach children Sunday school. But what if we look more closely at Noah's story as it unfolds, especially the scene where he becomes drunk and curses his grandson, a curse that Christians used for hundreds of years to justify slavery? What if we looked at this story as a way of talking about the impact of traumas on a family (a flood destroying the earth's inhabitants would surely have been traumatic!), and include in that discussion the ways traumas lead to family secrets and family interventions, and the importance of no longer covering up the actions of leaders who hurt others? In an era of #MeToo and ongoing clergy sex abuse scandals, it is important that we help people in churches stand up to authoritarian leaders and interpretations of the Bible that have been used to justify the misuse and abuse of power.

We want to take a deep dive into these stories that may be familiar, as well as those that are not, in order to talk about how these texts can serve as mirrors for some of the pain in our modern world. Returning to the idea of reading the text relationally, it is important that we see it not as a voice that speaks only of what God wants and intends. Rather it should also envision the text itself as a mirror of what is happening in our lives and as a testimony that God is still present in the messiness of it all. For families today who are struggling with moving for a parent or spouse's job, for example, perhaps they can listen to the story of Sarai and Abram and see the pain of their journey as something that enables them to talk in their own family about the difficulties of relocation.

Second, we want to give voice to the characters in these texts who do not actually have a voice in Scripture, and let these silences be a reminder to us today to listen to the voices in our own families that often are silenced. Sarai, when following Abram out of Ur, doesn't have a say in the matter. Similarly, there are couples today navigating moving cross-country or the world for one family member's job—either through corporate moves or military base relocations or educational opportunities. Sometimes members of a family feel that they do not have a voice in those moves. So connecting these two experiences—the lack of voice of the characters we read about in the text and the felt sense of lacking voice in the family that some family members may experience—can hopefully help create a bridge between the world of the text and the world of our families today, to deepen empathy and opportunities for discussion in and among family members.

Third, and this builds upon the first two goals, our goal is to help readers deepen their relationships and make more meaningful connections with their families and communities of faith. By making stories from the book of Genesis relevant to the lives of families today, and by practicing empathy with characters whose voices are silenced by the biblical narrative—as well as with family members who may experience their own voices as being silenced—we hope to create opportunities for persons to have conversations about their family relationships in ways that can deepen their connections and create a greater sense of care. Ultimately, we hope that readers can feel seen and heard by God and by others in their family by discussing experiences common to many families through the lens of the biblical text and by cultivating a deeper sense of empathy with and for one another.

These three goals, in summary, guide our work: helping readers find relevance in these biblical stories to the experiences of families today; creating opportunities for empathetic listening to voices in the text and in families; and encouraging readers to deepen their own familial relationships and connections with their faith communities.

Churches can become a family for many individuals, and it is important that these conversations about family—in the broad sense of human longing for connection—happen in churches where many families worship together and people join to find a place of belonging. We hope this book will be accessible to persons who are in small groups together, as well as a helpful tool for preachers looking to engage these issues from the pulpit. Whether you are reading this book alone, as a member of a family you grew up in, or with a family of your own today, we hope you will see and hear in these pages some of your experiences addressed. And in the way we talk about the text, we hope you will be able to engage more deeply with the relationships all around you: in your home, with your family of origin, and with the family that is your community of faith. Along the way, we hope you will deepen your relationship also with this text we call the Bible, strengthening your ability to challenge and question parts of it that seem harmful, as well as opening yourself up to the wisdom it still conveys. And ultimately, may your deepening relationships remind you of the constant and abiding presence of God, who does not need us to "work on" or "deepen" our relationship to God, but who is always already deeply abiding in us and through us, throughout our lives.

Chapter 1

Not Good to Be Alone?

Singleness and Breaking the Norm

SCRIPTURE: GENESIS 1:1–3:24

Introduction

The idea of "biblical families" may seem to conjure up some sort of traditional understanding of what it means to be a family: a man, a woman, and their children. Unfortunately, the church has too often painted this picture as the only way for people to be part of a "family," ignoring the fact that many people live in situations that are very different from that particular arrangement. The church is also a place where some people feel particularly left out if they are not married with children. To begin this discussion of biblical families, we want to challenge some of the ideas around "family" because there are many ways of being a family. We also want to name the ways that the church has at times harmed people who feel left out of traditional images of family.

So first, we study the story that started it all off: the story of Adam and Eve, where the Bible first says that it was "not good that the man should be alone" (Gen. 2:18). We look at this story to raise questions, and to consider whether the basic storyline is itself a message we are passing on in the wrong way. For instance, when churches assume it is "not good" for persons to be alone or to be single, we are sending a message that a "real" family is something different, when in reality persons who are single can tell us what it means to be a family just as much as persons in long-term relationships can. Or another example is how the church has used the story to paint Eve, and all women, as inferior to men. These are mistakes we want to avoid in retelling this story. And along the way, we want to question how these stories have influenced our own views of the family

9

and how we may need to shift in how we view one another. Let us begin with an in-depth look at the beginning of Genesis.

Families at the Beginning of Creation

Considering the dramatic plot and unforgettable imagery—a pristine garden paradise, forbidden fruit, a cleverly talking snake, and a devastating expulsion—the story that ends with humanity's exit from Eden is usually imagined as the *only* story about humankind's creation in the Bible. Yet unknown to most readers, this story is one of *two* different accounts of the creation of human beings and therefore of the first human family in the biblical corpus. The prominence given to the Eden story and to a particular commonly accepted interpretation of this narrative have greatly impacted the ways in which the church envisions human relationships, setting up a normative vision of the family that has limited the more complex ideas conveyed in the biblical text.

The First Story of Creation

Mesmerizing in its liturgical cadence, the Bible begins with the creation of the universe by an omnipotent deity imagined as a fluttering spirit and commanding voice (Gen. 1). Perhaps because of its hypnotic repetition of divine satisfaction, "it is good," as well as its neatly ordered day-by-day structure, most readers gloss over the first succinct narrative of humanity's creation that comes at the conclusion of this chapter. On the day before the first Sabbath, which finalizes God's great creative act (the Hebrew root, *shabat*, means "to rest, cease, desist" as well as "seven"), the biblical text states that God created humanity alongside all the other living creatures on the earth (Gen. 1:25–27).

The description of humanity's creation is simultaneously humbling and lofty. We are created alongside all the other earthly creatures and, as such, envisioned as no better than—indeed, as siblings of—the animals, creeping things, and beasts that are also divinely birthed on the sixth day (v. 25). This humbling description speaks to the deep interconnectedness of humanity with the other creatures that inhabit this divinely created world. This understanding in turn compels us to widen our vision of the family as one inclusive of other living beings that share this planet with us.

After declaring our familial place alongside other creatures, the text pivots to point out humanity's uniqueness by pausing to detail our creation:

"So God created humankind [*ha-'adam*] in its/his image; in the image of God, it/he created it/him; male and female it/he created them . . ." (1:27, author's translation). This single poetic sentence, which encompasses the first story of humanity's creation in the Bible, tells of how God created humanity—in Hebrew, *'adam*, a word related to the term for earth and soil (*'adamah*), and which later will be used as the personal name of Adam—in God's image.

This sentence, however, is packed with ambiguities and contradictions, the most important of which is the switch of pronouns at Genesis 1:27 from singular to plural in the Hebrew of the Masoretic Text (MT), which is the authoritative Hebrew version of the Hebrew Bible. Some translations, like the NRSV, might mention this switch of pronouns in their notes. In this verse, humanity is referred to by the singular pronoun in the first part of the sentence ("in the image of God, it/ he created *it/him*"), but switches to the plural in the second part of the sentence ("male and female it/he created *them*"). The fluctuations in the pronouns convey two significant points. First, this story explicitly states that males and females are created at the same time. If we assume that birth order conveys notions of hierarchy, the simultaneous creation of male and female strongly suggests that the genders are equal. Second, the concurrent creation of males and females has implications for the imagined gender of the creator deity. It suggests that the deity who created these first human beings might also encompass both genders. Going further, the fluctuations in gender even put forth the possibility that this creator deity is fluctuating in gender. This vision of the creator God as fluid, neutral, or complicated gender-wise is significant when we consider that humanity is said to be created in God's image (v. 27). If we are made in God's image, then we too might be more complex in gender than we presume.

These ideas that emerge from this first story of creation—that we, as human beings, reflect both our androgynous creator deity and also the beasts and animals that are created alongside us on the same day—open up space to enlarge our understanding of the family. A family need not necessarily consist of a male and a female and their children, as is typically imagined, but can consist of a more heterogenous and complicated grouping, such as that of a single person and their pet, or two friends. Indeed, even a single person in relationship with their God can be considered a family. The meaning and idea of family, in short, can be enlarged to encompass any group composed of creatures in relationship with each other or with their deity.

The Second Story of Creation

The second story of creation in Genesis 2:4b–3:24, usually attributed to a different source or group of writers, has a variant account of the creation of humankind. This second account initially appears to assert more firmly the bifurcation of genders: God states that it is not good for Adam, who is created first from the dust of the ground and assumed to be male, to be alone (2:18). However, God cannot find a fitting helper (*'ezer ke-negdo*) for this first human among any of the animals (2:20); this leads to the creation of the woman through the surgical use of Adam's rib; this woman will later eat the fruit from the tree of the knowledge of good and evil, leading to the expulsion of the first humans from the Garden of Eden.

Interpreters have taken the creation of the woman after that of the assumed man, the use of Adam's anatomy in her creation, and the woman's designation as a "helper" as indicative of the inferiority of the woman, and therefore all women. Yet, as Phyllis Trible has shown, there are significant problems with this argument.[1] The most prominent problematic assumption is that the creation of the woman after *ha-'adam* implies her subordination and deficiency. This assumption presumes that the first created being in the Eden story, designated as *ha-'adam*, or "the human," only encompasses one single gender: male. However, since the differentiation of genders does not occur until after Eve's creation and Adam's subsequent declaration of the intimate relationship between the two genders (2:23), the first being might have been androgynous, not simply male.

As to the order of creation, being created second need not necessarily imply inferiority. Rather, as evident in Genesis 1, creation climaxes with the creation of humanity on the sixth day and with God's rest on the seventh. Hence, the creation of the woman at the very end of God's creative act might indicate that she is the apex or culmination, not a subsidiary, of God's creative act. Equally dubious is the claim that females are inferior because of the woman's creation from a rib. This "method" of creation, Trible argues, is no better or worse than the creation of the first person out of the dust of the ground. Rather, considering that no other living creatures in the garden sufficed as a partner for the first human, there is a heightened sense of divine intentionality with the creation of the first woman, which again hints of Eve's superiority.

The fairest reading, however, is that the Eden story, similar to the first story of humanity's creation, also evinces a kind of equality between the two genders. When the woman is created, the man happily declares: ". . . this one shall be called Woman [*'ishshah*] for out of Man [*'ish*] this one was taken" (2:23). The wordplay between "woman" (*'ishshah*) and "man" (*'ish*) indicates that the two genders are intimately interrelated and interdependent. Indeed, notice that the woman is designated as a "helper befitting him" (*'ezer ke-negdo*) (2:18, author's translation)—with the term *neged*, which means "in front, opposite" or "parallel to," used alongside the term *'ezer*, which means "helper." Considering that is *'ezer* is a word frequently used to describe God (cf. Exod. 18:4; Deut. 33:26, 29; Pss. 121:2; 124:8), this description seems to imply that the woman, as a helper parallel to the man, is equal to him. Both the woman and the man therefore are equal partners in a mutually beneficial relationship.

Eating the Fruit and the Expulsion from the Garden

The supposed inferiority of the first woman, Eve, stems not only from the order of her creation but also from the fact that she has long been faulted—unjustly, we would argue—for the biggest theological failure in human history, referred to as "the Fall," an event that has come to be interpreted by some as the original sin. That is, Eve is the one who talks to the serpent and disobeys God by eating the forbidden fruit first and is therefore blamed for humanity's expulsion from the garden. Yet again a more critical stance leads to a better and richer understanding of this tale.

The deed that causes the expulsion—the partaking of the fruit, traditionally envisioned as an apple because the Latin word for apple, *malum*, is a near homonym to the Latin word for evil—is usually assumed to be negative. However, several hints in the story suggest that partaking of the forbidden tree might have been part of God's plan all along. First, God plants this tree smack in the *middle* of the garden, not in some shadowy, difficult to reach corner surrounded by a protective fence (2:9). Second, God, instead of hiding the tree, deliberately points out its location to the first human (2:17). Last, God heightens the temptation by telling the first human that they can eat of anything *but* of the fruit from that tree (2:16–17). If God does not want the humans to eat of that tree, then why does God point it out and make it more enticing by declaring it forbidden? Is this some sort of divine marshmallow test or a deliberate setup by God?

It is also telling that God informs Adam, but not Eve, that the fruit of the tree is very poisonous by stating that the eater will die on the day it is consumed (2:17; a statement that turns out not to be entirely true). If there is a poison pill in the garden, why doesn't God warn both inhabitants? Moreover, where is God when the serpent approaches Eve? Indeed, if Eden is so perfect, how did the serpent come to be in the garden in the first place? Why doesn't God clear the garden of dangerous trees and talking serpents before letting the children roam free? Could it be that God is aware of and indeed has allowed the serpent into the garden so that it can entice the humans to eat the fruit?

Indeed, to truly understand this narrative we need to clear away some of our presumptions about this story. The first concerns the serpent. Despite what the serpent comes to represent in the church, the biblical text neither equates the serpent with Satan[2] nor portrays it as evil or nefarious. Rather, the serpent is described in Hebrew as *'arum* (Gen. 3:1). Though this word is sometimes translated negatively as "crafty," it actually means prudent or sensible. Indeed, Proverbs repeatedly uses *'arum* to describe how a person should behave, that is, prudently and wisely (Prov. 12:16, 23; 13:16; 14:8, 15, 18; 22:3; 27:12). Moreover, in other mythologies, the serpent has a complex and powerful symbolism, signifying regeneration, eternal life, sexuality, boundary crossings, and chaos. Hence, in Genesis, the serpent is envisioned not as Satan or an evil being but as a kind of trickster—a clever boundary crosser that brings about a different stage in the development of the world.

The second assumption that we must rethink concerns Eve herself. Readers have sometimes assumed that the serpent approaches Eve instead of Adam because she was mentally or spiritually weaker and therefore more easily tempted. Yet again the text points to a different reading. Far from approaching Eve first because of some perceived defect, the prudent serpent might approach Eve instead Adam knowing that she was the smarter or more curious of the two. Maybe the snake even felt a bit sorry for this intelligent being. After all, the serpent is the first and only creature ever to speak to Eve directly. Perhaps the serpent speaks to Eve first because Eve seems so utterly alone, isolated, and bored. Perhaps the serpent was trying to help Eve by telling her how to escape her gilded cage.

Indeed, it is telling that the serpent, in contrast to God, not only speaks directly to Eve but has the audacity to tell her the truth: If she were to partake of this fruit, she would not die that day as God told Adam, but her eyes would be open like God's, and she would obtain knowledge. Isn't it good to want to have one's eyes open, to obtain knowledge, and to be like God? The assumptions that Eve should have just obeyed God's command as filtered through the man and that she should have hidden away her curiosity, her desire for knowledge, and her desire to be like God—don't these assumptions sound suspiciously like modern-day admonitions telling women they shouldn't demand education, equal pay, or access to certain jobs? That they should remain meek, mute, and proper?

Instead of interrogating Eve, let us instead turn to interrogate Adam. Where was Adam when Eve was speaking to the serpent? The text does not hide his whereabouts: "So when the woman saw that the tree was good for food, and that it was a delight to the eyes, and that the tree was to be desired to make one wise, she took of its fruit and ate; and she also gave some to her man *with her* and he ate" (3:6, author's translation; italics added). It appears that Adam was there in front of us the whole time—he was *with her*. But then if he was with Eve, why doesn't Adam say or do anything? Why doesn't he contradict the serpent, and warn and try to protect Eve? Why doesn't he knock the fruit from Eve's hands when he sees she is about to eat it? Didn't God tell him—and only him—that the fruit was highly poisonous, capable of bringing death on the very day that it is consumed?

It seems that Eve is not the only curious creature in the garden. Rather, Adam also appears to have been quite interested in the forbidden tree. Unlike Eve, however, Adam is unwilling to be the first to face the dangerous plant. He is, however, quite willing to use his new partner, Eve, as a taste-tester. By letting Eve eat the fruit first, Adam can make sure it not poisonous and also blame Eve if they are caught. And indeed, this is precisely what he does do when God confronts him: "The woman whom you gave to be with me, she gave me fruit from the tree, and I ate" (3:12). No wonder the phrase that Adam was "with her" in Genesis 3:6 is often left untranslated and even missing in some translations of the Bible. For example, this phrase is missing from the fourth-century Latin translation of the Bible called the Vulgate as well as modern translations such as the Revised Standard Version (RSV) and the 1985 translation by the Jewish Publication Society (NJPS).[3]

This story has several implications about how we should envision the family. According to this interpretation, the Eden story is about the failure of partnerships, and in particular, about the failure of the first man, Adam, to act as a "helper befitting *her*," that is, as an equal and supportive partner to Eve. This story illustrates isolation and neglect, especially in familial situations. It is, in part, about the general mistreatment or neglect of partners and dependents. This story is also about the unfair blame placed on women for things that go wrong in the family. It is about relationships that go awry and families that become dysfunctional. It is about how these familial problems begin from the very point human beings are created and are forced into a relationship with each other and with their God.

Finally, this story is also about the ambivalence that parents feel about their children and their progression into adulthood. As I noted earlier, there are some hints that God wanted Adam and Eve to eat the fruit and leave the garden. Indeed, after they partake of the fruit, they are clothed, understand sexuality, have babies, and have to work for a living (3:16–21). The text nowhere describes the partaking of the fruit as a sin or envisions the aftermath as a curse. The aftermath is not a curse. It is not the Fall. It is life as we live it with all its complexities, beauties, and horror. What happens after Adam and Eve eat of the fruit is that they grow up, become socialized, and move out of the house.

If we imagine God as the parent, what does God want for the children? Does God want them to partake of the tree of eternal life, that is, remain forever as children, with their eyes closed, never exposed to good and evil? Or does God want them to grow up, move out of the house, and become fully formed adults even if they might make terrible mistakes and suffer for them? If God is a parent, then I think God simultaneously wants both these things and neither of them. God is likely deeply ambivalent and torn. This second story of humanity's creation is therefore not about "the Fall" of humanity, but about the beginning: the beginning of human society and history, and therefore the beginning of these ambivalent groupings of people in relationships called families.

Talking about Adam and Eve Today

With all of this rich material to draw from, where do we start in having a conversation about the story of Adam and Eve and how it impacts our relationships with our families today? There are many issues in this story related to families: singleness, notions of sexuality, gender roles, and the power of origin myths in shaping our idea of what makes a family. In the spirit of looking at the text relationally, we can examine this story's influence on our ideas about family relationships, and we can choose whether or not we want it to exert the same kind of influence on us today. Because our relationship with God is different from our relationship with this text, we can bring before God our challenges and questions that we have of the story. We are also freed to examine this text in its larger context: as a story meant to tell us about the beginnings of the world and to point to God as the Creator of all things, and not necessarily as a story that dictates the shape of all families for all times. Furthermore, by looking at the story next to other cultures' origin myths, we can see how other relation-ships are lifted up and celebrated in ancient sacred literature and imagine for ourselves what implications that might have for families.

Theme #1: Our Origin Myth Is One among Many

How does the story of the beginning of Genesis function in the larger story of Christianity? This text begins with the words "In the begin-ning," so in many ways, it starts off the whole story. These first few chapters form the Christian origin myth. To use the word "myth" is not to say the story is not true. Popular usage of the word "myth" associ-ates it with falsehoods or deliberate untruths. But in the story form of a myth, myths create meaning and significance for persons who hold these stories as important. If you cannot shake the link between myth and falsehood, substitute a different term in your mind, such as legends or stories of creation.

The start of any story is important; even more so for stories that have helped us make sense of our place in the universe and the world we live in, stories that place us in the larger context of time and space with a universal "In the beginning. . . ." Whether or not we take the first three chapters of the Bible as literal, the stories about the creation of the world and the creation of humanity shape how we view ourselves, others, and the natural world. Particularly, if we emphasize one part of our origina-tion more than another, then the part we stress becomes more central to our sense of identity. For instance, understanding ourselves as being made in the *imago Dei*, or the image of God, tells us that humans are special. We are unlike any other part of creation. Basing our identity in this part of our origination story, we emphasize that something sacred is embedded into who we are. Of course, this can also have a negative effect on how we view the world. Seeing ourselves as closer to the divine than animals or the natural world, we have tended to devalue and degrade the quality of the earth we live in.

The origin myths of other cultures and religions provide points of comparison for how humans have tried to locate their origins in some supernatural being(s) calling forth the first humans. In the *Popol Wuh* (or Popol Vuh), a myth originating with the Quiché or K'iche' people of Guatemala telling the Mayan story of creation, the beginning of time starts with the presence of the Heart of Heaven forming all that is in the earth and sky.[4] Along with two other deities, the Heart of Heaven cre-ated all the animals, but none of them could praise their maker. So the gods tried creating people to praise them, and they started by making humans out of mud, but they turned limp and dissolved in water. Then, they created humans out of wood, but the people did not have minds and could not praise their makers. Finally, the gods decided together to make people out of corn.

The creation of people in the *Popol Wuh* is also interestingly similar to the creation myth in the Bible. There are accounts of the creation of all people (the original materials being mud, then wood, and finally, corn), followed by accounts of actual people who are known as named ancestors. In this second thread of narrative, the deities that govern Hell are wicked and cut up a being who has preceded the creation of humanity—Hun Hunahpu, who along with his brother, Wukub Hunahpu, "were born in the darkness of the night, before man was created, and before the Sun and the Moon existed."[5] When the Lords of Hell tricked Hun Hunahpu and his brother and chopped them into pieces, they put them in the ground. But the head of Hun Hunahpu they placed in the branches of a barren tree by the road. "As soon as the head was placed there, it disappeared and the tree gave forth fruit. . . . The Lords of Hell thought of this tree as something miraculous and ordered everybody to keep away from it."[6]

When I first stumbled across this book of myths when I lived in Arizona, I was struck by the similarity between this special tree that gods tried to keep others away from, and the tree of the knowledge of good and evil found in the second chapter of Genesis. The tree in the Garden of Eden sounded strangely similar. The story also involves a woman breaking with the will of the gods to approach the tree. Yet the woman in the *Popol Wuh* is not disobeying the Heart of Heaven, she is going against the Lords of Hell. And when she disobeys and approaches the tree, her daring boldness enables her to receive a gift that leads to the creation of heroes. Consider how the story sounds similar to what we read about in Genesis.

In the *Popol Wuh*, a woman known as Xquic, one of the daughters of the Lords of Xibalba (translated as Hell), became curious when a tree that once had been barren began to bear fruit. This tree is known as the Calabash, or gourd tree, and it creates fruit that is as big as a human head.

> When she saw the tree full of fruit, she said to herself: "I shall not go without tasting one of these fruits. I am sure I shall not die." She was thinking this when the head that was placed in the fork of the tree said, "Do you really want of this fruit with all of your heart?" "Yes, I want it," the maiden said. "Stretch out your right hand,"

said the skull. Xquic extended her right hand, and straightaway the skull let its spittle fall into the maiden's hand. When she looked at it, nothing was on the palm. The skull said: "The spittle I threw to you is the mark of my descent that I leave to you. Go, walk up to Ulew, the Earth, and you will not die." All this was accomplished by the order of Hurakan, Chipi Caculha and Raxa Caculha, who are the Heart of Heaven.[7]

Xquic gave birth to two sons, Hun Ahpu and Xbalamque, who become the heroes of the story by defeating the Lords of Hell. Xquic raises her sons by escaping to earth and moving in with her mother-in-law, the mother of the slain Hun Hunahpu, whose head was in the tree. Xquic and her mother-in-law together raise the boys Hun Ahpu and Xbalamque.

This may seem like a strange coincidence. The translator of the original *Popol Wuh* during Spanish colonization was Father Ximénez, a Dominican priest. It may be that some of the story shared with him resembled stories that he would have been sharing from the Bible. It is not clear how the stories came to resemble one another so closely. Other early mythologies similarly have things in common with our early biblical narratives, such as the *Epic of Gilgamesh*, which includes a flood story similar to that of Noah's ark.

Comparing the biblical narrative to the *Popol Wuh*, they both entail two different types of creation: the first story describes the creation of humanity in general, and the second story, specific characters. The Bible has God creating humanity in God's image in chapter 1 of Genesis, followed by a specific account of God creating Adam out of dust, and subsequently Eve out of Adam's rib. The Mayan story has humanity created out of mud, then wood, then corn, followed by a specific story of the creation of particular people. Rather than Eve being tricked by a serpent to eat of the forbidden tree, the Mayans have Xquic boldly approaching the forbidden tree, hearing the voice from within the tree, and receiving spittle that makes her conceive of the ancestral heroes Hun Ahpu and Xbalamque, and she travels to earth by escaping the Lords of Hell. One woman is tricked, the other is courageous. One woman is banished from idyllic Eden, the other escapes from Hell. One is cursed to endure pain in childbirth, the other is miraculously impregnated. One was created to be a helpmate to Adam and has been treated as his inferior, the other was born of deities and gives birth without the help of any man. Consider the impact of growing up in a culture where the story of Eve is the origin myth for the beginning of women and the image of the first family compared with a society in which Xquic stars in the origin myth and becomes the first mother of humanity and lives in a family with her mother-in-law and two children, without a husband. How differently would the two societies understand the value and capabilities of women? Or how would they view differently the role of women in the family?

Considering other origin myths can help Christians to reimagine our own myths that have left us with archetypal images of what it means to be a woman or a man, and what it means to be a family. Could reevaluating our origin myths in light of other ways of thinking about the first humans help us think in new ways about what it means to be a family? In the Mayan story, for instance, Xquic is a single woman. She is not married. She raises two children with the help of her children's grandmother.

Talking about origin myths can help all of us consider our own archetypal expectations of what it means to be "family." Who do we picture when we hear the word "family"? What images of family did you grow up with? What kinds of configurations get included when we talk about family? And how does singleness play into these conceptions?

Theme #2: Questioning Gender Roles

Just as the Mayan origin myth helps us consider the different archetypes for family, this early text in Genesis provides an opportunity to question our paradigm of gender roles, helping us to detangle the messages the church sends about gender. First, looking at both of the creation stories in Genesis—the first, where God creates male and female in God's image, and the second, where God creates Adam from dust and Eve from Adam's rib—we need to ask our congregations which story has had the bigger impact on our own understanding of gender. Bringing together both of these stories, we can begin to critique older interpretations that read these texts as determining gender roles as something God-ordained and set for eternity.

As mentioned in the biblical commentary above, the use of pronouns is particularly complex in the first creation story. The pronoun for God changes from singular to plural, exactly when God is said to create *them*— male and female. Because both men and women bear God's image, there must be something of the feminine as well as the masculine in the person of God. With discussions of gender fluidity today—acknowledging the diversity of ways persons can experience themselves as gendered—it is important to preach about a God who sometimes goes by a different pronoun—a God who goes by *they*, and a God who is reflected in both male and female, encompassing both. If God's image includes both genders, who are humans to suggest to one another that we are all only ever *one* thing? Persons who identify as transgender or genderqueer do not identify with the gender of the biological sex they were born with. Some persons may let us know the pronouns they wish to go by. Some persons may never tell us they are transgender. In churches, you may not know who has a child at home who is considering transitioning or who themselves are transgender. Talking about God in a way that demonstrates the gender fluidity within the person of God can help persons who are genderqueer or transgender to know that they, too, are made in God's image.

Secondly, we need to be able to critique biblical interpreters that focus solely on the second creation story to justify the subordination of women. Drawing from the exegetical discussion of Eve earlier in this chapter, it is important to challenge our basic assumptions about what this story about Eve says about women. Can we reclaim a more positive understanding of Eve, rather than indicating her as the cause of the Fall and the source of all suffering? Perhaps we could experiment with retelling the story from Eve's perspective, imagining the internal thoughts that may have crossed her mind. Rather than using the word "helper" or even "help meet" (for those who grew up hearing the King James Version) to describe women, words that suggest women are subordinate to men, perhaps we could remember that this same word in Hebrew was also used in the Bible to describe God. Adam and Eve as the first couple have unfortunately been set up as an archetype by persons who want to argue that men and women were created differently and for different purposes, and that because of this, they should have different roles in the home and in society. As Christians, it is our job to challenge this way of interpreting the text and invite one another to consider how men and women alike are called to be in relationship and at work in the world, caring for God's creation.

Theme #3: The Role of Singleness

In Genesis 2, after God puts Adam in the garden and tells him not to touch the tree of the knowledge of good and evil, God declares, "It is not good that the man should be alone" (v. 18). Messages across history and cultures have communicated to people that they need to be coupled, and that it is not good to be alone. Yet in Paul's writings, he declares that it is better to be single (1 Cor. 7), and celibacy has been a required part of the priesthood for centuries within the Roman Catholic Church, which suggests that the church has supported singleness as a vocation.

Also, the verse that follows God's declaration that it is not good for the man to be alone is the verse describing God bringing all of the animals to Adam to see what he would name them. What if we saw this as a way of acknowledging the human-animal relationships that happen with pets and other creatures? What if our discussions of family included the furry or feathered friends that many people consider members of their family? What if we read Genesis 2:18 and God's subsequent action of bringing the animals to Adam as a sign that God intends for us to be in relationship with the rest of God's creation? That we should care not only for members of our immediate human family but also for the birds of the air and the fish in the sea?

Do you know people who have pets who can share stories of how these animals have changed their lives? More and more research shows that animals have many things in common with humans, with some being able to recognize faces, demonstrate intelligence, and even display signs of grief. Persons with pets may tell you the ways they have seen these capacities at work in animals. And, the feelings are often mutual. Birders, persons who go out looking for birds, can recognize the calls, shapes, and colors of birds in the same way that they remember a human face.[8] We connect with animals in ways similar to how we connect with other humans, and it is important that we consider animals as part of our larger family when talking about our interconnectedness as God's creation.

What do we mean when we call someone "single"? We may use it to describe people who are not in an intimate or romantic relationship with another person, or people who are not yet married. Often, the sense the word carries is all in the *"yet"* before married, carrying with it the assumption that marriage is the ideal state for all persons, and singleness is somehow just a preliminary stage one must wait through. It is important the church not repeat this error of attribution, using the label of "single" to highlight someone as not-*yet*-in-relationship. Instead, we need to acknowledge that everyone who is in this way "single" is also connected to others through ties of family, friendship, and in the case of animals, through deep bonds with the pets in their lives. Whether an individual decides to pursue a romantic relationship is entirely up to him or her, and has nothing whatsoever to do with whether they are "alone." A person can be not in a romantic relationship and entirely surrounded by community and deep bonds of kinship at the same time. The opposite is also true: a person can be in a romantic relationship while also feeling alone and isolated from others in the community. Singleness does not imply aloneness.

Theme #4: Implied Sexuality

"God created Adam and Eve, not Adam and Steve." Thus say Christians who argue that gay sexuality is against God's original design. How can there be other forms of sexuality if God only created man and woman at the beginning? The claim is an attempt to make this origin myth define human sexuality for all time.

Just as we should be cautious in seeing the Adam and Eve story as the primary origin myth that guides our understanding of what it means to be family, so should we be cautious in presenting this couple as the archetype of human sexuality. By implying that God's design focused on men and women reproducing, we place an undue emphasis on heterosexual couples with children as somehow living out God's plan for humanity. God's plan was for all to be able to experience the goodness of creation, and to glory in the goodness of God. Persons who are gay, lesbian, bisexual, transsexual, or queer are all expressions of God's good creation, and the way they live out their lives in fruitful ways testifies to the generosity and creativity of God, who continues to give us blessings in new and unexpected ways, who unites us in families that we may not have imagined for ourselves. In the myriad ways that people can be "fruitful," each person has the capacity to continue in the act of creation that God began, and that may be as persons who live in intimate relationships with persons of the same gender, opposite gender, or persons who choose to live in relationships that are non-intimate. Human sexuality does not define how persons model the image of God; the *imago Dei* is already present in each and everyone.

Questions for Reflection

1. Who do you picture when you hear the word "family?" What images of family did you grow up with? What kinds of configurations get included when we talk about family? And how does singleness play into these conceptions?
2. What gender is God usually imagined to be, and how does this affect our relationship with God, family, and our faith communities? How do these relationships with God, family, and community change if we imagine God as encompassing both genders or as fluid in gender?
3. What impact does the misinterpretation of the Garden of Eden story as being about Eve's subordination and blame for the Fall have on our churches and families? If the creation stories in Genesis

are reimagined as depicting gender equality, as argued here, how would this change our families, churches, and communities?

4. In light of other ways of thinking about the first humans, how can we reevaluate our origin myths so that they can help us think about what it means to be a family in a new way?

5. The two creation stories undoubtedly concern our relationship and the family's relationship to animals and the natural environment. What experience with nature or animals, be it family fishing trips or having a pet, did you experience as a family, and how do they affect your family?

Chapter 2

Brothers' Keepers

Sibling Rivalry and Violence

SCRIPTURE: GENESIS 4:1–16

Introduction

Like many stories in the Hebrew Bible, the tale of Cain and Abel, which constitutes the first story of sibling rivalry and violence in Genesis, centers on a peculiar feature of humanity and of the human family: our rivalrous and jealous nature and the ways in which it can lead us to inflict violence upon each other. The story ponders why we treat each other badly, even going so far as to kill each other, even though we are all part of the same human family. Going further, the story also questions the role of God and religion in the fracturing of familial relationships.

The Rivalry of Cain and Abel

Shortly after Adam and Eve are expelled from the Garden of Eden, the biblical text describes the conception and birth of Cain: "Now the man knew Eve, his woman, and she conceived and she bore Cain. And she said, 'I have acquired a man with YHWH'" (Gen. 4:1, author's translation). This description is unusual. Instead of naming the father, it says "the man," *ha-'adam*, knew (knowledge being a common metaphor for sexual relations in the Bible) Eve. This word, *ha-'adam*, as evident in the English transliteration, consists of the definite article plus the word *'adam*, which can refer to a man or to humanity in general. The term is also used as the personal name of the first human being, Adam. However, the inclusion of the definite article, "the," makes it difficult to think that the personal name is meant here, as "the Adam" makes little sense. However, if Adam is not the father, who is? Who else could Eve have

25

"known"? If we follow the chronological trajectory of the Bible, at this point, Eve and Adam are the only humans on earth.

Equally strange is Eve's exclamation when she gives birth that she has *qaniti*, usually translated as "acquired" or "obtained," "a man with the help of the LORD." Aside from wordplay on Cain's name—pronounced as *qayin* in Hebrew—the use of this verb is strange as it links Cain with the acquisition or obtainment of possessions. Continuing the mystery, Cain, who presumably is a newborn, is oddly designated "a man"—a man who somehow is the result of YHWH.

The plain reading is that Eve is stating that God is the one who helped her have a male child. However, these strange verses have led ancient biblical interpreters to posit some fascinating interpretations. They argue that the odd manner in which Cain's birth is described shows that, even as a child, Cain was not normal. Indeed, his abnormality was the result of his mother's misbehavior and his corrupt heredity. Cain, they argue, was the product of adultery. Who is Eve cheating on Adam with if there are no other human beings around? Well, it must have been with the devil either in the guise of the serpent—the same serpent that caused such havoc in the Garden of Eden—or in the form of an angel. This is why Eve states that the Lord, which interpreters reinterpret as implying "an angel of the Lord," had something to do with Cain's birth, and why the text designates Cain's father as not Adam, but "the man."[1]

Whether you agree with these interpretations or not, the blame for Cain's future violence falling on his abnormality, his mother's misdeeds, and faulty heredity—that is, Eve's adulterous affair with a bad "man"— parallel modern explanations of violence or misbehavior. How often does society blame someone's actions, especially violent ones, on deficient upbringing or an unfit mother (mothers usually take the brunt of the criticism)? How often is heredity touted as the root cause of someone's misconduct?

Whether true or not, these explanations of human violence, both ancient and modern, show that interpreters had difficulties explicating and understanding human violence. They cannot explain what led Cain to kill his own brother and, indeed, going further, what still leads people to kill each other even though we are all members of the larger human family. By arguing that Cain is literally the seed of the devil, this question about our violent tendencies is mollified with a theological explanation that leaves the real question about violence open and unsettled.

Indeed, the narrative, through wordplay on Cain and Abel's names, offers other explanations as to the causes of familial discord and human violence. Cain's name in Hebrew, depending on how the sounds and letters of his name are configured, sounds like the words for "to be jealous, envious" (*qana'*), "to acquire or purchase" (*qanah)*, and "to subdue" (*kana'*) or "oppress" (*hiknia'*). Cain's name also sounds like the word for a dirge or a lament (*qinah)* as well as a rare word for weapon, lance, spear, or something pointy (*qayin)*. Abel's name, pronounced as *hevel*, in contrast, sounds like the word for breath, vapor, or mist (*hevel*)—that is, something that is fleeting and momentary; something that disappears and dissipates. Indeed, it is onomatopoeic in that the term, which means "breath," mimics the sounds we make when we breathe or sigh. Abel's name also, tellingly, sounds likes the word *'avel*, which means "to mourn" or "to fade."

Through the different connotations of these names, the story hints that familial rivalry, jealousy, oppression, and violence are partially the result of our greed, desire, and envy: that is, our need to acquire and obtain things that our sisters and brothers have. Jealousy and envy, many times, lead to fighting and violence: that is, to forging and using weaponry. And the end result of all this is death or the dissipation of someone's life, and laments and dirges to mark this disappearance. Jealousy over and desire for what the other has is so powerful, the text hints, that it can cause us to forget that we are all related to each other, that we are all family.

The Role of God in the Sibling Rivalry and Violence

It is not just economics and desire, however. Rather, this story also offers a theological explanation of human violence by depicting God as playing an outsized role in the breakdown of the relationship between the two brothers and the intrafamilial violence that follows. God looks at Abel's gift of the firstlings of his flock and the fat with regard (v. 4), while mysteriously disregarding Cain's gift of the fruit of the ground (v. 5). Realizing that Cain is disappointed, God proceeds to make him feel worse, telling him that he did something wrong without clearly explaining what it was and then mysteriously warning him to behave himself (v. 7). Considering God's insensitive response to the unhappy Cain, it is unclear whether God was trying to look out for Cain or trying to goad him into more irresponsible behavior.

Considering further the frequently problematic portrayal of God, a common explanation is that Cain must be to blame for God's disregard of his offering. God can't be unfair, can't be to blame, so someone else has to be at fault. The statement that Abel offered the "firstlings of his flock" (v. 4) is interpreted to mean that Cain's offering was inferior or second-rate—that is, not the firstling. However, the text nowhere states the exact nature of Cain's misdeed. Moreover, Cain is said to have been a farmer, and while the firstlings of animals have symbolic resonance in the Hebrew Bible, there is no such thing as the firstling or fat of fruits.

The search for Cain's wrongdoing therefore stems from the need to understand and justify God's behavior. Without an explanation, God appears unreasonable, unfair, and insensitive, arbitrarily favoring one gift over another, and in so doing, one person over another. God never clearly explains to Cain what he did wrong, and instead of comforting Cain over his hurt and jealous feelings, tells him that he should improve himself somehow—not very helpful! Most problematically, God, knowing of Cain's disappointment and how he might behave as a result of it, never warns Abel or intercedes when the conflict between the siblings turns violent. God, in short, is portrayed as a pretty bad parent.

Lest we think that our world is far removed from that of Cain and Abel, we should recall that we still reside in a deeply unfair world—a world in which one person or group is haphazardly favored over another. What in the ancient world was interpreted as God's favor, in our world is called the luck of birth. In our world, some people are born with the "right" appearance, skin color, gender, and sexual orientation. Some are born in the right country at the right time with the right amount of money and socioeconomic standing, while others are not; and those who are not are frequently made to feel worse—indeed, outright blamed—for their situation. They are sometimes told, just like Cain, to buck up, to do better and to not screw up without clear instruction, help, or compassion. By depicting God's favoritism as one of the causes behind the conflict between Cain and Abel, the story argues that injustice and inequality—the luck of birth—and the deep anguish that stems from them are also partially responsible for the rivalry and breakdown of familial relationships and the violence that sometimes ensues.

Indeed, God is not the only character who is insensitive to issues of inequality. Most translations of the Bible, such as that of the Greek, Syriac, and Latin, fill in the dialogue between Cain and Abel at Genesis 4:8. However, the authoritative Hebrew version of the Hebrew Bible, known as the Masoretic Text (MT), leaves the dialogue between the brothers blank.[2] We don't know what the two brothers said to each other right before Abel's murder. The absent dialogue opens up interpretative possibilities. Elie Wiesel, the Nobel Prize–winning writer and Holocaust survivor, imagines Cain trying to tell Abel, his brother, about this grief and his emotional pain. Abel, however, pays little attention and is not very empathetic, refusing to even listen to his brother. Perhaps he even revels in his favored status.[3] In this reading, though Cain is the one to inflict violence, he is not the sole culprit of familial discord. Rather, compassion, attention, and sensitivity, especially on the part of those favored and blessed by God, are shown as a necessary bulwark against the fracturing of the human relationships in the family.

Making Sense of Sibling Rivalry in Our Contexts Today

In considering ways to interpret Cain and Abel within a larger study focused on families of the Bible, several avenues unfold as possibilities for discussion. The first is to point to the social conflicts within society at large that tend to separate us into groups of us versus them. Beyond rivalries that pit New York Yankees fans against the Boston Red Sox or our favorite college sports teams, is there a "sibling rivalry" that runs so deep in our world that the animosity toward the "other" does not end at the end of a sports season? If we look at Cain and Abel metaphorically, standing for the larger factions dividing the world, this text can help us consider the causes and sources of discord, as well as the deeper pain that results from our interconnectedness as one human family. This text could be a jumping-off point to talk through ways we value the gifts of some and not others, the rivalry and competition we feel toward other groups or countries that can lead to violence and war, and the sense of disconnection we feel for the fate of others, asking "am I my brother's keeper?" Questions to ponder along this line of study might include: Who are the groups we feel the least amount of responsibility for? Who are the people we envy because we perceive their gifts as more valued by society? How can we individually and collectively recognize our connection to the larger human family?

A second avenue would be to look at the local level, considering how in our organizations, institutions, and churches, we can fall into a form of "sibling rivalry" where we seek the approval of leaders, jealous of those who seem to receive favoritism from those in leadership. If you are reading this as a pastor, consider how your congregation perceives your friendships and the support you give certain members or groups within the church. Is there a way you can address the feeling of sibling rivalry and celebrate the gifts of all members of the congregation? The same could be true if you are reading this as a leader of an organization or institution. Which groups within your institution need more of your attention?

How can you help foster a greater sense of familial connectedness across the organization? A good way to help persons feel heard is to encourage persons to meet with you as your schedule allows, because a face-to-face meeting can often resolve disputes and mistrust. If you are a member within these organizations or congregations, and you feel the dissatisfaction of having another member or group taking priority over your own needs and interests, it can feel a lot like someone is choosing the gifts of others over those that you bring. It is really crucial for people who feel overlooked to remember that the gifts they bring are indeed good in and of themselves, despite the lack of recognition afforded by others. Cain's gift was not bad in any way, an offering of fruit and harvest, that for some mysterious reason was not accepted as Abel's gift had been received. This is often the way it feels to be in the world—one person succeeds while another fails, though both possess equal gifts and capacities. While sometimes we may suspect discrimination at work—racism, sexism, ageism, or other forms of oppression—it is not always easy to prove or to call out. In those cases, it is important to retain the dignity of one's own sense of giftedness, time and time again, not letting the messages of the world determine our own sense of value. At the same time, this could be a good time to talk more about the various forms of oppression that make the overlooking of some people and their gifts more prevalent.

A third way to reflect on this text is to link it to the context of actual families, a case where parents see their own children experiencing sibling rivalry and competition. Because this work is focused on "families," this final connection may be the most obvious to readers of the text. We read of two brothers, both who had given gifts to God, but only one who received God's blessing and approval. The resulting resentment ended in violence and death. Two brothers, one driven by jealousy, destroyed the other.

For parents of young children, reading this text may represent their worst nightmare, in which one of their children harms the other, perhaps violently so, and perhaps with deadly consequences. While the scenario of one child murdering the other may seem far-fetched, consider the development of a parent's relationship with their children, and how unintentional changes in that relationship over time can foster resentment.

With the first child, parents develop a close and connected relationship with their "only," helping the child feel attached to a loving caregiver, where parents experience love for this child that was previously unknown to them. When considering having another child, the parents may not think anything could change this relationship with their firstborn. But of course, having another child changes everything.

Immediately upon having a second child, the relationship between the parents and first child goes through changes, while the parents and firstborn must both adjust their expectations. A newborn requires constant care and interrupts the parents' sleep schedule, leaving the parents exhausted and unable to spend the same kind of time with the first child as they could before the new baby arrived. The firstborn can no longer enjoy unlimited access to the body and comfort of the parents. While snuggles and hugs could previously be shared at any time, now it is the newborn who has privilege of place in the parents' arms and laps. And now, instead of welcoming the firstborn into an embrace, the parents may push the child away to avoid the child smothering the newborn.

So the seeds of sibling rivalry are sown long before the siblings are old enough to fight with one another. The first child sees this other child, their sibling, as an intruder, an interloper, a rival who has successfully won the love and affection that the firstborn previously enjoyed alone and full-time. As much as parents can try to remedy this early separation of the children into competitors, perhaps by spending time with the older child, giving books to explain the changes that come with a new baby, or giving a special gift just for the older child, nothing can permanently ease the pain experienced by the first child in "losing" their parents to another child. These feelings may show themselves through apparent aggression toward the other child, or in more subtle forms like escalating patterns of irritation. The parents, noticing the older child being too rough or squeezing the baby too tightly, learn to keep an eye on the siblings' interactions, aware of the danger to their newborn that their older child presents.

As the children grow, the older child and younger sibling may take turns serving as irritants to the other. Petty fights can turn into angry outbursts, and someone inevitably ends up in tears. While one child may not be intending to murder the other, for parents observing their children's constant fighting, this pattern of behavior is deeply troubling. Sibling rivalry or perpetual fighting can turn a home into a house filled with tension and negativity. What can parents do?

First, it is a good idea not to follow the example God sets in the text. For whatever reason, God delights in Abel's gift, and rejects Cain's offering. Parents should do their best not to overtly praise and value the talents of one child over and against that of the other child. A parody of this kind of treatment appears in the television show *The Good Place*, where the parents of one of the main characters, Tahani, pit her against her sister Kamila. The scene shows their parents telling the two sisters

as children that they are going to paint for a competition—one painting will be featured in the main hall during their evening party, and the
other painting will be used for fire kindling. Of course, just as in every
other competition Tahani enters with Kamila, she loses yet again to her
talented, adored, and favored sister.[4]

Of course, most parents do not try to torture their children in this way,
and yet still their children fight with each other nonstop. Is there another
glimpse of hope here for parents exhausted by their children's fighting?
Perhaps the mystery in the text is also a way through the sibling rivalry.
Just as we do not know why God rejected Cain's offering, so too, we
do not always know why our children are fighting. Perhaps resentment,
jealousy, and competition are the source of their conflict, but perhaps
there are other reasons. Sometimes children are mean to their siblings
when they themselves are feeling bad or sad or tired. Taking out negative
feelings on others can be a way children deal (unsuccessfully) with these
difficult emotions. Finding ways to help your children self-soothe, and
being willing to openly accept their feelings, can hopefully help them
contain their feelings and allow children to accept themselves.

Another way to respond to sibling rivalry is to acknowledge to your
children that it is painful for you to see them fight, and to share with
them your own experiences (if applicable) of sibling rivalry. You might
say to your children: "I see you both really upset at one another, and I
remember what it felt like to be in a big fight with my sibling. It did not
feel good. So I'm sorry you both are having to go through this right now.
It's painful, and I'm sorry you have to experience this. I wish I knew how
to make your relationship easier for you both, but that is something you
will have to figure out for yourselves. But I want you to know how much
I love each of you, and that I'm here for you." This does not solve the
rivalry, but it does provide an opportunity for children to see themselves
through another's eyes, and to recognize the suffering that they are going
through in fighting with one another. By promising to love your children
through their fighting and suffering with one another, you are providing
a witness to the unconditional love that God has for all of us.

That unconditional love of God is the good news of this text, hidden
within a latent promise. Such a promise involves the larger narrative arc in
which God continues to care for humanity, even when humanity remains
embroiled in violent conflict within itself. This promise, that God continues to be with humans and care for them, is one sign of hope for readers of this text: here is an example of humanity at its worst, and yet God
still provides. For parents worried about their children, remembering the

provision and providence of God can help parents entrust their children into God's hands.

Now, given Abel's death, this may not feel like good news since God does not apparently prevent Cain from killing his brother or warn Abel about the impending attack. But this text reminds us that we cannot control our children, and we cannot prevent them from harming others—intentionally or unintentionally. We can do what God does in the text, cautioning them to watch their behavior and to not let their jealousy get the better of them. But telling our children how to behave is different than how they actually behave. No amount of parenting wisdom can make our children immune from developing resentment against their siblings. But we can entrust our children to God's care, praying for them, and doing our best to accompany each of our children on their journeys through life.

Questions for Reflection

1. What are the ways our society (or your church or community in particular) tries to make sense of violence?
2. Who are the modern-day equivalents of Cain and Abel? And how does this story help us empathize with and understand today's Cains and Abels better?
3. How and where do you see "sibling rivalry" play out in your own communities? And how can we address such feelings of rivalry so that we can celebrate all the gifts in our communities?
4. If you have children or grew up with siblings, what has been your experience with the sibling rivalry of childhood? If that rivalry has extended into adulthood, what are possible avenues for reconciliation, if any?
5. Where is God in our rivalries? How can we better trust in God with our children and with our own gifts so we can do our own part to help heal our divisions?
6. How can we individually and collectively recognize and indeed strengthen our connection to the larger human family?

Chapter 3

Trauma and Family Interventions

Noah and His Family

SCRIPTURE: GENESIS 6:5–9:28

Introduction

Most of us, especially those of us who grew up attending Sunday school, know about the famous Noah: the builder of a giant boat, the babysitter to the world's animals who come to him two by two (at least in one account of the flood), and, most notably, the survivor of a giant worldwide flood. What is not usually remembered or discussed is what happens to Noah and to his family—a family whose existence is also usually forgotten about—after the flood. We know they survive, but how does this disaster affect them as individual characters and, most importantly, as a family group? Moving from the text to the world, how do such traumas, be it worldwide natural disasters or personal ones, affect us, especially in the ways that we relate to each other? With these questions in mind, despite being remembered as a tale of survival, it is best to recast Noah and his family as a story about something darker: trauma and the lingering shadow it casts on the individual and the family unit.

The Survival of Noah and His Family

The story of Noah's family begins in Genesis 6 and takes up a great deal of literary real estate, ending at Genesis 9. This story about the survival of Noah and his family during the great flood, like the narrative about Cain and Abel, is mythic and ahistorical in nature. That is, the writers were less concerned with history and more interested in telling a story that they felt contained truths relevant to their readers' lives. In short, there are messages in this tale that go beyond whether Noah was a real

35

man or whether there was really a big boat or a flood that was universal in proportion. And some of these messages seem to center, as is often the case with stories in Genesis 1–11, known as the Primeval Narrative or the Primeval Story, on families and familial relationships. Of particular concern here are the effects of disasters and trauma on the family unit.

And there is much to traumatize Noah and his family. Genesis 6–9, which consists of two different accounts of the flood that have been merged into one, describes how Noah and his family—namely his wife, three sons, and their wives—are the lone survivors of a cataclysmic, world-wide flood. The story hints of what we now call "survivor's guilt" on the part of Noah and his family. Indeed, ancient interpreters also raised questions about the story, which, incidentally, are the same ones that plague survivors of traumatic events today: Why should Noah and his family be alive at the end of the story when no one else was?[1]

This question is particularly relevant because the biblical text is rather cagey about the exact reason why Noah out of everyone on earth was the lucky recipient of God's instructions and plans on how to ride out the deluge. Indeed, the biblical text itself seems to present two slightly contradictory reasons why Noah (and his family) made it out alive while the rest of the world drowned. The first is that Noah was just lucky; he mysteriously found favor or grace in the eyes of God (6:8). The second explanation, perhaps added by editors/writers who felt that just being lucky was theologically unsatisfactory, state that Noah was not just lucky but really, really good: "Noah was a righteous man, blameless in his generation; Noah walked with God" (6:9). Yet this second explanation, likely meant to clear up the first explanation, raises more questions than it resolves. The description of Noah's goodness is incredibly bland and general. If Noah were so good—indeed good enough to be the sole survivor of a worldwide catastrophe—what specific examples are there of his exceptional goodness? Indeed, as I will discuss in a moment, his later interaction with his son actually hints that Noah might not have been very good at all, and certainly, not so good as to be designated as the sole survivor of a divinely ordained cataclysm.

Indeed, considering the supposed goodness of Noah, his lack of questioning God is deeply problematic. When God tells Noah that the entire universe is going to be destroyed, why does Noah—supposedly, the best person on earth—not try to stop God? If a mass murderer tells you of his plans, even if the murderer is God, is it not a moral duty to try to stop the assailant instead of remaining silent and passive? Indeed, the story with its vague explanations—the flood killed everyone because everyone was very bad (Gen. 6:5–7), except for Noah who was very good (6:9)—practically begs the reader to ask questions. How is it possible that everything—every baby, child, or animal—was deemed deserving of death but not Noah and his immediate family? And how can anything, even if the entire world was so thoroughly corrupt and bad, justify an act of worldwide annihilation?

Not only does the flood kill every human and animal, but it is envisioned as an enormous ecological disaster. All the trees, insects, and flora were wiped out as well. If we currently are disturbed by scenes of giant swaths of forest being burnt down by fires, hurricanes leveling cities, and floods submerging entire towns, the global deluge is worse than all these natural disasters combined. Indeed, the biblical text describes the flood as God releasing the floodgates—that is, windows or slots on the top and bottom of the universe—and letting the chaos that surrounds the universe flood into the created world (Gen. 7:11). It is, in short, portrayed as the undoing of God's creative act in Genesis 1 where God ordered the universe and limited the chaos so as to create a bubble of the living in the midst of chaos and death.

Equally troubling as Noah's response to being told about the flood is his silent and passive reaction after the flood. If Noah is so good, how can he not question God and God's goodness *after* the disaster? He and his family have just witnessed the mass death of every child, baby, and animal, which were not fit to be taken into the ark. If he did not question God before the disaster, shouldn't Noah challenge God after the catastrophe? If Noah is a good man—so good in fact that he is the only one that deserved to be rescued by God—then shouldn't such a good person question the motivations, the ethics and the goodness of a deity that would commit mass murder and destruction of the entire universe on a whim? Shouldn't witnessing such an event have shaken him to the core—made him question whether this God was really worth worshiping?

Disasters, Trauma, and Abuse

To be fair, my questioning of Noah might be a bit undeserved. There are certainly more empathetic ways of reading this character. When viewed through the lens of trauma, there are indeed some hints in the text that the flood, as many disasters do, had long-lasting effects on Noah and his family as a whole. The first clue is the silence of Noah and each of his family members—the silence which, as I noted above, is odd and uncomfortable. Noah and his family after the flood never speak about this event; they never question God. Indeed, it doesn't even appear that they talk to each other very much at all. It is as if they are in complete and utter shock. Rather, once the flood ends, the first thing that Noah and his family do is build an altar to God and establish a new covenant with the deity.

Their actions are rather telling. To be sure, they are thankful to be alive, but their altar building might not simply be out of gratitude. Rather, it might stem from a sense of fear, appeasement, or dread. Indeed, the silence too might stem from a place of terror. Perhaps no one says anything or challenges God because Noah and his family are deathly afraid of God. Noah and his family, according to the contours of the narrative, are alone in the world, which they now know after the flood seems likely to be ruled by a genocidal, short-tempered maniac. Like a child or a spouse stuck in an abusive situation, perhaps Noah and his family are so silent and passive because they are terrified of again triggering this abuser's violence? Perhaps they are silent because they are numb, traumatized, and scared.

Indeed, the marker of the covenant or agreement in which God promises Noah and his family that God will not use the flood to destroy everything next time (notice that this promise contains a rather large loophole) is marked by a sign—a kind of sticky note, reminder to God consisting of a "bow in the clouds" (9:16). This bow is usually taken to be a rainbow. And though a rainbow seems like a rather gentle and pretty sign, remember that the Hebrew word does not say rainbow, but a bow in the sky. And a bow is not really quite as lovely when we consider that it is, especially in the context of the ancient world, a weapon—that is, it is a tool used to kill things. Hence God's posting of this sign is akin to God flashing a gun to remind himself (and I am using God with the male pronoun here because in most cases in the Hebrew text, God is imagined as a male deity) to check his murderous ways. Indeed, it is hard to know whether this sign is a reminder or a threat. If the frightening image of God as a destroyer was not obvious enough in this story, God promises never to murder again (with water) by flashing his weapon. If Noah and his family were not already traumatized enough into silence, they certainly are with this threatening gesture.

Considering this encounter with God, it seems likely that the text is hinting that the reason that Noah and his family survive is because of dumb luck. For some reason, the person with the gun decided not to kill them during his murder spree. Noah and his family survive while others don't, *not* because they did anything special or because they were more pious or ethical, but because they were just plain lucky. This explanation, however, is a difficult one to accept because it means that their lives, and by extension, ours, are not ruled by order but chance and whim; or even worse, as the story of Noah reminds us, our lives might be under the control of something more chaotic and utterly unknowable. Noah and his family at the end of the flood are never told why God has chosen them to survive, and they are left with a sense that God could and indeed might reverse his decision at any point. It would also make sense that aside from a sense of trauma and shock, that the characters would also feel, as we would feel in a similar case, a keen sense of survivor's guilt, and with it, the attendant feelings of depression, existential malaise, irritability, helplessness, and numbness.

The Aftermath of the Flood

There are indeed other signs of trauma aside from the utter and befuddling silence on the part of Noah and his family. Notice what Noah does immediately after his terrifying conversation with God. He plants a vineyard, makes wine from it, and drinks so much of the wine that he lies around in his tent naked (9:21). That the text mentions Noah's drinking after such a catastrophe like the flood again hints of underlying psychological pain as substance and alcohol abuse are linked to abuse and trauma.

The story gets more disconcerting from here. As Noah is drunk and lying around in his tent, he is discovered by one of his sons, Ham, who tells his other two brothers about his father's sorry state. These brothers, Shem and Japheth, then walking backward and covering themselves so as not to look at their father, enter the tent and cover their father's nakedness (9:23). A deep sense of shame runs throughout this story. Thus far, this story is understandable enough, however, if not a little dark. Indeed, though we have to take care not to reduce the biblical text into a simple instruction manual, the actions of Noah's sons cannot but bring to mind modern interventions for alcohol abuse. And according to this reading, the biblical text in its description of the careful and respectful way that Shem and Japheth approach their father—as compared perhaps to Ham's response—might provide some general hints on how to approach and intervene when a family member is in distress.

If so, however, Noah's response to this "intervention" provides a stark example of how not to respond; or perhaps, it is an example of some of the negative reactions that one might encounter when such an intervention is staged. We are told that when Noah wakes up, he somehow knows what his youngest son (9:24)—that is, Ham—had done to him, and then curses *Canaan*, Ham's child (9:25–27), with perpetual slavery. Noah then blesses his other two sons, even okaying the future enslavement of Canaan's descendants by those of Shem (9:27). To understand the significance of Noah's reaction, it is important to keep in mind that blessings and curses, especially in the biblical context, were not idle jibber-jabber, but something that had real force. This was especially the case when this speech stemmed in the form of a curse or blessing from a patriarch, such as Noah. In short, this angry declaration from Noah was not just a meaningless outburst, but something that had long-lasting, *real* effect. It was something that came to fruition.

There are many questions about Noah's response: Why is Noah so upset when Ham seemingly just looked at him? Is looking bad enough to condemn the descendants of Canaan, his grandson, to perpetual slavery? And if not, then what exactly did Ham do? And why is Canaan, and not Ham, targeted by Noah? What is this curse of Canaan about? For the sake of brevity, I will quickly summarize some of the scholarly responses to these questions. As apparent from Noah's over-the-top response, Ham's view of his father's nakedness might have entailed something more than just "looking" as we understand it today. For example, some argue that looking on someone's nakedness in a patriarchal context such as the ancient Near East would have been a mark of deep disrespect to the elder man, especially to a patriarch, and as such, Ham's action was more egregious than we would think of it now.

Other scholars argue, however, that "looking upon the nakedness" might be a euphemism for inappropriate sexual relationships. That Noah is drunk adds to the sexual connotations of this story as wine and drunkenness is sometimes connected to inappropriate sexual activity (cf. the story of Lot and his daughters in Gen. 19:30–38). Hence, some interpreters have argued that Ham's misdeed of "looking upon the nakedness" might have entailed Ham taking advantage of his father or of his mother, as sometimes a woman's body and access to it were referred to as the nakedness of her husband (cf. Lev. 20:11). If Ham's act entailed incestuous relationships with his mother, then this would explain, in part, why Noah curses his grandchild, Canaan, who might have been a product of this incestuous relationship.[2] Some interpreters go in a different direction, however, and argue that the blame on Ham and Canaan is a cover-up for child abuse, even perhaps child sexual abuse, on the part of Noah, the parent.[3]

The problem, of course, is that the text nowhere spells out what exactly is going on, and this lack of clarity is likely deliberate. The writers and editors of the Bible were not neutral—indeed, most storytellers are not. Rather, they had a complex agenda, and one of these agendas was political. Notice that the main person mysteriously targeted in this story is *not* Ham, *not* Noah, but Canaan and Canaan's descendants who are cursed with perpetual slavery. And Canaan (and his descendants) are not just nobodies to the writer, but rather were the Israelites' archenemies. Why was that? Elsewhere the Bible claims that the Canaanites were particularly sinful, but that explanation leaves a bit to be desired. The real problem with the Canaanites was that, according to the biblical text, they were already dwelling and settled on the land that the Israelites wanted for themselves when they showed up there after the exodus. Subsequently, as the stories in Joshua narrate, the Israelites went to war with the Canaanites for that land and took it from them. In short, there was a political reason why the Israelite writers/editors might have wanted to make Canaan and his descendants the "bad guys" of this story in Genesis. It was a way to justify Israel's later conquest and enslavement of the Canaanites.

Considering this rather sordid history, it is fitting (though no less disturbing) that the curse of Canaan would be later used to justify the enslavement of African Americans in the United States. Though the history of the interpretation of this curse is too complex to explain fully in this limited space,[4] this misinterpretation stems, in part, from the genealogical lists that follow this story in Genesis 10, whereby Ham's descendants, namely Cush and Egypt, refer to lands and nations that were located in Africa. However, Cush and Egypt, both countries, which were respected and at points feared by the biblical authors, though descended from Ham, are not Canaan. It is Canaan and not Cush or Egypt that is mysteriously cursed by Noah with perpetual slavery in Genesis 9:27. Hence, the curse of Noah, deliberately misinterpreted to uphold an unethical institution, would indeed continue as a lingering curse, infecting other people and other nations.

In terms of the family, the sad way that this story concludes with Noah's drinking, the family intervention, the fracturing of family relationships, and Noah's cursing of his own family members shows that this family was undone and deeply affected by the disaster they had lived through. Despite the positive way that Noah's story is often remembered, when read more carefully his is a dark narrative of the effects of trauma on the family in the aftermath of a calamity. It is also a tale about the tragedy of the entire human family—those who were not saved like Noah—who, though not innocent, were neither likely to be so wicked as to merit a divine death sentence. In a time of global climate change when more natural disasters are predicted, we would do well to think about how these disasters will strain the bonds of kinship, be it in small family units or the human family as a whole.

Talking about Noah Today:
Trauma and Family Interventions

Perhaps by this point you are deciding to scrap any discussion of Noah and his family. They are too complicated. Too traumatized. Too political. And yet, if we let Noah's family tell us different stories than the simple one that we learned as children, then those new stories may prove helpful to the many complicated and traumatized families we know today.

It might be best to look at this story over the course of a few weeks, rather than all at once. The story of the flood and Noah's family's survival of this natural catastrophe can be by itself an avenue for talking about natural disasters in contexts where persons in your community have themselves lived through floods, fire, or other major storms. More and more people around the country and across the world are still rebuilding after storms or natural disasters that took place years earlier. How does the trauma of living through a storm impact personal and familial relationships for years afterwards?

Living with family trauma, different members try to put their lives back together in their own way. Noah took to gardening, planting a vineyard, and then drinking. In modern families, members may pour themselves into their work, or try to heal from their wounds by self-medicating through drugs or alcohol. People often turn to addictions to nurture themselves after a painful time; and yet, far from healing our hurts, addictions open wounds of their own in a cycle of separation and self-destruction.

In such situations it is important to distinguish between the trauma that first affected the family, and later forms of trauma that keep perpetuating harm within it. For instance, it was not Noah's fault that the flood came and wiped out the entire world. But his act of cursing Canaan was a new trauma that he inflicted upon the rest of the family system. This is why it is so important for family members to attend to their own experiences of pain and loss; denying their own pain, they are more likely to inflict that pain upon others. Had Noah gone to God to express his anger at God for the destruction of the world, perhaps Noah could have dealt with his pain in a less destructive way. Perhaps he would not have lashed out in anger at Ham's son, who was innocent.

Separating the original trauma from subsequent traumas is important. They both need to be addressed and named so that persons can heal, but it is challenging to address them both at the same time. This is because natural disasters are traumas that do not obviously carry blame. While we may want to discuss climate change and talk about political inaction and its negative impact on our environment and ensuing catastrophes, on another level there are plenty of crises that families experience that are nobody's fault. Many terrible things can happen to a family where no one can be blamed. And yet, families respond to crises in ways for which they later must take responsibility. For instance, if a family member gets struck by lightning, it was a freak accident. But if another member responds to that trauma by entering a downward spiral of drug addiction, that requires another conversation. Both things are traumatic for the whole family; but the first event cannot be blamed on anyone, while the second relates directly to choices the drug-addicted member is making. A family intervention may be necessary to help that person change course.

Family Interventions

What happens when one member of the family is self-destructing and harming others in the family as well? In the case of Noah and his sons, Ham noticed that Noah was passed out drunk and naked. The other brothers decided to cover Noah so no one else could view their father's nakedness. Right here, we have two approaches to family interventions: Ham's approach was to notice that something was wrong and to tell someone else about it. Shem and Japheth's approach was to cover everything up, including their father's nakedness. Perhaps they were embarrassed and did not want anyone to know, especially if their father was a renowned patriarch. Perhaps they thought they were doing the right thing.

This text can help us imagine the challenges of talking about problems many families face today: alcoholism, domestic violence, mental illness, drug addictions, or child abuse. If one member of the family notices that something is wrong—that another member is a threat to themselves or to another person—then how should the observer react? Who can they tell? Clergy are mandatory reporters in most states, which means that if they become aware of someone who is an immediate threat to a child, then they are required by law to report that situation to the appropriate authorities.[5] Knowledge of child abuse makes us complicit in that abuse if we fail to report the abuse to law enforcement.

But what if the situation is not clearly child abuse? What if a family member is frequently drunk, or seems to be taking drugs, or otherwise appears to be making choices that are self-destructive? What would this passage from Genesis lead us to do? If we were Shem and Japheth, we might be tempted to try to cover it up, to try to keep others from knowing about it as best we can, hoping the situation will resolve itself with time. Perhaps we feel powerless to change the situation, so we do our best to manage outward appearances and to minimize the damage to the family this individual is doing. Or, like Ham, we go and tell someone. But judging from how Noah reacts, it seems like following Ham's lead would only get us into trouble.

How many people in our communities have struggled with dealing with family members who behave inappropriately or self-destructively? How many people in our churches know personally the trauma that comes with internal feuding among families about what to do with the problems created by one or more people in the family? My guess is that there are more out there than we know.

And the challenge of this passage is that it seems to condone Noah's behavior. It seems to give a pass to the cruelty exhibited by Noah's curse on Canaan by letting this curse later justify the conquest of the land of the Canaanites. For persons who call out another family member's bad behavior, there is rarely a sense of victory. More often than not, the person doing the callout receives anger, resentment, and denial on behalf of the person behaving badly, as well as from members of the family who would rather cover the whole thing up.

Edwin Friedman, a Jewish rabbi known for his work on family systems theory and how it applied to church and synagogue contexts, emphasized that congregations and families were their own "systems," and like natural systems seek homeostasis or the status quo. The reason why families are the way they are is because they "work." While they may not work equally well for everyone, there is an internal logic to families that makes them run the way they do. That is why, according to Friedman and other family systems thinkers, it is nearly impossible for a single person to change his or her family. It is too hard. If a single person tries to take on the system, the homeostasis of the system will be threatened, and so the system will fight back with everything it has to try to keep that individual back in line. Ham's pointing out Noah's nakedness is the challenge to the system. Noah's curse of Ham's son is the pushback.

The advice Friedman gives to persons wanting to change the system is this: change yourself. The technical term is "differentiate," which means to make yourself into something different from the system itself. As each of us acts on the system, we are actually activating the system and becoming more and more a part of it. But when we differentiate ourselves, that is, work on ourselves and our own personal growth and goals, then we are changing the system by not contributing to it in the same way that we have in the past. Rather than reacting as we usually would to the system, supplying the system with energy it needs to survive, we can conserve our energy by letting go of our attachment to our previous ways of interacting with others in the system and focus our energies on our own development as individuals.[6] If we change the ways that we behave, we may not change the system in the ways we want it to change, but the system will inevitably be different, because *we* are different.

But the bad news for people who want to try to address problems in their families is that the family seldom responds to interventions in positive ways. Noah curses Ham, and then Noah lives another three hundred years, and the descendants of Ham include the Canaanites, the Philistines, and Ninevites: all enemies of ancient Israel. In fact, this little vignette in Genesis 9:20–28 seem to be the backstory for an entire who's who of biblical bad guys in the rest of the Hebrew Bible. Assyria? It gets mentioned in the section of Ham's descendants (Gen. 10:11). Sodom and Gomorrah? They are there too (10:19). Why were all of these folks the enemies of God's people? The reason is right there in Genesis 9:20–28! It's all because Ham pointed out to his brothers that their father had gotten drunk and ended up naked.

So our choice as readers is to decide whether to keep this story hidden, or to point it out to others. We have our own intervention to make: bring this terrible story into the light of day, or walk backwards out of the room, covering it up as if we never even saw it happening.

The silence over this story is familiar to us—much like the silence over family secrets that are too embarrassing to name or too distressing to address. There are many stories like it in the Bible. They are stories that are just a little too much like us: complicated, awkward, not showing us at our best. In the same way, the history of the church has seen one cover-up after another. Child sexual abuse by clergy in the Roman Catholic Church and other denominations is but one of many abuses the church has been complicit in, and time and again the preferred response has been to cover it up.

But we have choices. We do not have to cover up the bad behavior of Noah or our loved ones or the institutions we hold most dear. In fact, we are living in an era when more and more individuals are saying #MeToo and coming out of hiding and naming the abuse they have experienced. The church has not been a safe place for many people, and if we have any hopes of being people who follow in faith a God who joined us by living in flesh and who spoke up on behalf of the oppressed and the abused, then we need to find the courage to speak up and out about the abuses still going on all around us. It is not going to be easy, and we may even receive more pushback from the system, but we have to do something if we want to change the world we live in. Changing the systems starts with changing ourselves: refusing to stay silent, refusing to cover up for other people's bad behavior, and refusing to become complicit in other people's abuse by our silence and inaction. The flood has already come. There are people suffering traumas. Let us choose to live our lives well, with courage, love, and honesty. We can take the first steps by being honest about what we read in Scripture, and not trying to cover it up.

Questions for Reflection

1. How does the trauma of living through this "act of God" impact the personal and familial relationships in the story in Genesis?
2. What does this story tell us about how people sometimes respond to trauma, both as individuals and as a family?
3. In what ways does our society (or your church or community) try to make sense of natural disasters? And how are these ways helpful or harmful?
4. How does this story relate to other stories that you may know about how persons have tried to respond to self-destructive family members or situations?
5. What stories need to be shared more openly in your own situation—your family or congregation, or the society at large? Are there stories of how people are responding effectively to intervene in family systems that you can share with others to encourage one another today?

Chapter 4

Trailing Spouses (or Family Moves)

Abram and Sarai's Story

SCRIPTURE: GENESIS 12:1–20

Introduction

Abram, who is later called Abraham, becomes the first patriarch of Israel, and the father of the three Abrahamic monotheisms—Judaism, Christianity, and Islam—as a result of his emigration to a country promised to him and his descendants by God. As such, migrations and movements are not only at the center of Abrahamic call, but at the center of the story of the chosen nation of Israel in the Hebrew Bible/Old Testament. Hence, in the account presented in the Hebrew Bible, emigration and migration are envisioned as divinely ordained and a necessary part of the salvation history described in the text. What is often forgotten, however, is that Abram does not travel alone. Rather, going along with him, and therefore, also impacted by God's call and the family's move, is his wife Sarai, later called Sarah. Even more than Sarai are the usually unnamed servants and slaves—including a slave woman of Sarai called Hagar—who also would have been given little choice but to move with her employer and/or owner, Abram. The world described by the ancient text might sometimes seem unfamiliar to us. However, a person's move or relocation still has a significant impact, albeit a little less dramatic, on the person's family and significant other, affecting both the person who decides to relocate and also the one who chooses to remain behind.

The Call of Abram/Abraham

Abram's story and therefore that of Sarai, his wife, appears to start rather abruptly without much of an introduction. Out of the blue, God calls

47

on Abram to move from his country, kindred, and father's house (Gen. 12:1). Considering the brevity of the biblical text, which is usually succinct, the repetition of the place that God calls Abram to move away from—his country, kindred, and father's house—indicates that Abram's separation is to be utterly complete and final: Abram is to leave behind everything and everyone that he knows, never to see his homeland or birthplace again. As Nahum Sarna notes, there is an ascending quality to this—country, extended family, and nuclear family—as he is asked to make increasingly greater and more personal sacrifices.[1]

The finality and the sacrificial aspect of Abram's move can also be interpreted metaphorically as an injunction against regression or even nostalgia, which is a kind of psychological returning or regression. Though one can look back on the past with regret, sorrow, or fondness, an inability to move beyond one's past or an attempt to go back to the past or change the present so as to coerce it to mimic or copy an imagined past is seen as regressive, dangerous, and outside the desires of God. Indeed, myths from the ancient world, including the story about Lot's wife who looks backwards and is turned into a pillar of salt in the midst of the family's flight from the destruction of Sodom and Gomorrah (Gen. 19), act as a warning against this overly indulgent backward look, whether literal or metaphorical.

Abram is known and lauded for his unquestioning movement forward, a movement that leaves everything and everyone he knows behind so that he can go forward to a mysterious place that God has yet to name, but promises to show the patriarch at a later time. Abram's action forward, based only on the elusive direction by God, has been interpreted as indicative of this patriarch's faithfulness and piety. Despite not knowing where he is going, what is going to happen to him, or even why he is called by God so suddenly, Abram listens to and heeds God's call. Indeed, in the ancient context, moving away from one's family and homeland entailed more than just relocation, but was in reality a matter of life and death, given the absence of police forces, lit roads, or emergency medical services. In these circumstances, the family or clan was a person's main source of protection and safety. Hence, Abram's unquestioning obedience to God's sudden command to immigrate reads as a courageous leap of faith and trust.

Yet as stated before, what is usually forgotten is that Abram does not immigrate alone; and if he is to be lauded for his faith and trust, how much more laudable are those who go with him, sometimes at an even greater risk than the divinely called patriarch? While Abram at least gets to speak to God directly, God never talks to Sarai, Abram's wife. This is despite the fact that God's command to move affects not just Abram but also his spouse. Moreover, while Abram is promised blessings and support by God for his act of obedience (Gen. 12:1–3), Sarai is promised none of these things. Indeed, neither God nor her husband ever talk to her—or at least, the biblical text describes no such conversation—before they embark on this radical and seemingly dangerous move to another unknown country. Yet the dangers of such a move for Sarai, as a woman, were greater. If the moving party were attacked, not only could she be killed, but she could have been raped or taken as a slave. Indeed, immediately after they move, the vulnerability of Sarai is evident when Abram's group is forced to go to Egypt, and she is quickly taken into the harem by the pharaoh (Gen. 12:10–20).

Moreover, the physical dangers for both Abram and Sarai were considerable—indeed more so for Sarai being that she was a woman—because they were both quite elderly. Abram is said to be seventy-five when he gets his call (Gen. 12:4), and Sarai is described as a decade younger (Gen. 17:17) when they embark on their trip. That God chooses a senior couple to fulfill the divine plan presents both problems and opportunities. According to the biblical text, you are never too old to be called by God, be it to become a minister or to start a new job or to move to a whole new town or country. That God has no age requirements with regard to the divine plan is simultaneously heartening and also rather terrifying. Apparently, God can upend your life no matter how old or how settled you are. These events would certainly have been frightening for Abram. They would have been even more so for Sarai, who is never spoken to or encouraged by God directly but who was expected to silently follow Abram to an unnamed place as the patriarch undertakes his call.

Finally, adding to the dangers for Sarai was the fact that she was childless—or most important in this context, that she was without a son. She had not given birth to a male heir of Abram by the time of the move, and as such, if Abram—her elderly husband—were to have died on this trip, she would likely have been unable to inherit as a woman and therefore probably would have become destitute. Away from her homeland and from her family, she would have been unable to return to her father's house and to seek protection from her brothers or male family members. With Abram's death, therefore, Sarai might have very quickly gone from a matriarch to a servant, slave, or homeless vagabond in a foreign country.

Hence, though Sarai's feelings are never inquired of by God or Abram, and, most problematically, are never mentioned in the text and never deemed worthy of notice or mention by the biblical writers, all of whom were almost certainly men, this move would have been even riskier for her than it was for Abram. And as such, she deserves more praise and renown for her act of faithfulness and trust. Abram just had to trust God who spoke to him directly. Sarai, on the other hand, had to trust her husband and her husband's claim that he had heard God correctly. She therefore also had to trust a God who could not be bothered to talk to her. Though faith is not a contest, the person who has more to lose is likely the person who has claims to a greater faith.

The Incident in Egypt

Indeed, there are some hints that the faithfulness of Abram was not as superlative as it initially seemed. At first, Sarai and Abram's migration goes smoothly. They head toward the land of Canaan, passing by famous locations along the way (12:6–9), before running into trouble when the land is struck by famine (12:10). As a result, they are forced to turn away from the promised land of Canaan toward Egypt, the breadbasket of the ancient Near East, in order to ride out the famine. In part because of the fecundity of Egypt, the biblical writers stereotyped the Egyptians as overly interested in sex—the story of Potiphar's wife being a prime example of this stereotype (Gen. 39). It is this stereotype that seems to undergird Abram's strange plan for Sarai to lie about her status as his wife when they reach Egypt.

Because Sarai is beautiful, Abram is afraid that he, as her husband, will be killed so that she can be taken into the harem. That Sarai is sixty-five here and deemed so attractive as to jeopardize her husband's safety offers a refreshing contrast to our modern, youth-centered notions of beauty. To save his own skin, therefore, Abram asks Sarai to lie and say that she is his sister, which she does, but is taken into Pharaoh's harem anyway. Abram, however, as Sarai's supposed brother, is not killed but treated very well and even paid off with gifts and riches, such as animals and slaves. This situation continues until God inflicts Pharaoh's house with plagues as punishment for taking Sarai into his harem. When Pharaoh becomes aware of Sarai's real status, he confronts Abram, and lets the traveling group continue on its journey (Gen. 12:10–20).

Needless to say, the story of Abram and Sarai takes a decidedly disturbing turn when they arrive in Egypt. The portrayal of Abram is especially distressing as the patriarch is shown as not only lying about Sarai's identity but also as prostituting his own wife, exchanging access to her for material gain. Also disturbing is that Abram seems to have grown rather rich by it and seems generally unperturbed by the situation. Indeed, it doesn't appear as if Abram was in a hurry to end his lucrative scheme until God barges in and punishes—not Abram—but Pharaoh and puts a stop to it. These actions undercut the portrayal of Abram at the beginning of this chapter as a paragon of faithfulness and piety. If Abram is so faithful as to blindly follow the directives of an unknown God to emigrate to another land, why doesn't Abram ask the same deity for help instead of concocting a plan to lie about his wife in Egypt? After all, the deity who called him to relocate likely would have been willing to help him out of this conundrum.

More distressing and problematic—again—is the silence of Sarai. Her feelings are never inquired about, and her well-being does not seem to have been much of a concern for her husband. Considering that Sarai is put into the harem, it is possible that she was subjected to rape and sexual abuse. Indeed, it is not just her husband's reactions that are lacking. The modern reader also wishes for a more sensitive reaction from God. Though we would like to believe and interpret God's punishment of Pharaoh as resulting from God's concern for the sexual abuse of Sarai, it seems more likely, considering God's lack of communication with Sarai before this incident, that God intrudes because of her status as Abram's wife, not out of care for Sarai herself. Indeed, the biblical text supports this reading by emphasizing Sarai's status as Abram's wife or literally his "woman," right after stating that God inflicted Pharaoh and his household (Gen. 12:17). As apparent, it is Sarai's status as Abram's wife—and therefore as a property of the chosen male patriarch—that leads God to intercede on her behalf. It is, notably, not necessarily her distress or suffering.

Sarai's reactions and feelings as well as her experiences as part of the harem in Egypt—whether she was mistreated or raped and whether she felt powerless or afraid—are all left glaringly unstated in the biblical text. Also unmentioned are her feelings about her move away from her family, her country, and her birthplace. How did she feel about leaving everything and everyone she knew behind? Was she able to adjust to her new location? Did she also feel called somehow? As evident from the silence, her feelings and her reactions appear to be of little concern to her husband or her God, neither of whom engage in any meaningful discussions with her. They also appear to be rather irrelevant to the biblical writers who wrote her story and claimed descent from this matriarch.

The silence on the part of female characters is one of the more difficult aspects of reading the biblical text as a modern reader, especially as a female reader. The lack of voices raises interesting questions and concerns about faithful readings and interpretations. How can we simultaneously acknowledge the text's authority and yet also recognize its limitations? Is there a way for modern readers to reclaim these silent voices without overriding and manipulating the text? These are all questions and concerns that current interpreters and reader have to wrestle with as they make the leap from this ancient text to the modern world. The best we can do is to become careful listeners of whispers and silences. Only then will we be able to hear the small, still voices of the women, children, the poor, and the marginalized who call to us from the spaces between the words of the Holy Scripture.

Modern Interpretation for Trailing Spouses

As we listen to the silences in Scripture, we begin to attune ourselves to the silences in our contemporary contexts as well. In a global economy, persons are working at jobs that take them around the world. Corporations that conduct business in several countries have employees who literally travel the world. U.S.-based multinational corporations employed 42.5 million workers in 2017.[2] How many of those workers moved to a new city or country for their jobs? In 2019 in the United States as a whole, there were around 157 million workers.[3] How many of those workers are working in the same town they grew up in? If you are reading this as a pastor, you are more than likely not working in the same place where you grew up. Educational prerequisites that we need for our jobs lead us to new cities so we can get the education we need to get the job we want. If you are a pastor, you probably went to seminary in a city different from the place where you grew up, and before that, you most likely attended a college or university that was also in a different location than your hometown. Speaking of "hometowns," it is becoming increasingly rare that a person today can point to a single town as their hometown, since so many families are moving around for jobs and education. Kids grow up having to move to different schools in different cities as their parents follow career paths to new locations.

How do families manage these moves? One good idea is to *not* follow the example of Abram in Genesis 12:10–20. In other words, do not pass your spouse off as your sister in order to court favor with the people in your new town. Joking aside, we need to let the blatant disregard of

Sarai's perspective in this story be the alarm signal to call our attention to the needs of trailing spouses and families. By focusing on the insensitivity of Abram in this text, we can learn from these mistakes and try not to replicate them today.

Taking Turns, And Staying Together: The Story of Kyle and Nelis

Whenever two people commit to be together for life, they each enter into the risk of having to move. And yet not every couple enters the relationship with the same fierce commitment that Ruth shows to Naomi later in the Hebrew Bible, declaring, "Where you go, I will go; . . . there will I be buried" (Ruth 1:16–17). When couples today follow each other for new jobs, it can feel stressful and frightening, and can lead to conflict in a marriage and in the family. One of the ways families navigate the modern employment situation is to take turns or to follow one spouse as he or she takes a new job in a new place, and then follow the other if and when the time comes for the other spouse to take a new job.

Let me introduce you to two people who have navigated the journey of moving for one spouse's career. Kyle is a Presbyterian (PC(USA)) pastor, and Nelis teaches statistics at a university. Kyle is from Texas, and he has a subtle southern twang when he speaks. Nelis is from South Africa, and he speaks with an accent that to unfamiliar ears may sound British. They are a gay couple, recently married, both living out their own vocations. Recently, Kyle left his job to move to the same town where Nelis had a new teaching job, and so I interviewed them about their experience of discerning their shared vocation as a couple. Their story is a treasure of sweet insights and deep resonance for how all of us can better attend to one another in the process of following out our calls.

Kyle and Nelis met in College Station, a small college town in Texas. As Nelis explained, they were just good friends at first, but they both had a sense that they could have something more than friendship. But life took them in different directions. After three years in College Station, Nelis got a job teaching in Dallas, which was three hours away from Kyle in College Station. At that point, they were just friends.

But after they moved to different towns, being three hours apart, the distance between them sparked a realization: how much they valued each other's presence and how much they brought to each other's lives. Thus, they entered into a long-distance relationship.

Not long after that, Kyle took a job in Austin. The distance between them was still three hours, but the drive felt easier, since now it was all on an interstate highway. They continued to commute to see each other for six and a half years.

Throughout that time, Kyle served a church in Austin and Nelis taught in Dallas, and they traveled regularly back and forth to be together. Kyle said that "for good or for ill, we got used to the commute." Nelis added, "We definitely got used to it, but looking back to it, we can probably identify areas in our relationship that suffered because of it, and not just our relationship." Nelis described how challenging it is to try to invest in a community of friends in one town, when you are constantly going back and forth between two cities. He said their friendships suffered as a result, since so much of their time was spent traveling to see the other.

They also lacked a sense of stability. Neither city felt truly "home," since they were often not together in the same place.

All along, they were waiting for something to feel more permanent and steady—for Nelis to get tenure, or for them to get jobs in the same city. But then, tragedy struck.

On April 17, 2018, Nelis was flying on an airplane from New York to Dallas when an engine failed. The plane started shaking and oxygen masks dropped, and a window, one row in front of him across the aisle, blew out. The plane had to make an emergency landing, and the woman who had been sitting by the window died. It was traumatic.

Kyle learned of the plane's engine failure while Nelis was still in the air, and Kyle reached out for support on Facebook, asking his community of family and friends for their prayers. He updated his page as soon as he learned that the plane had successfully landed in Philadelphia and that Nelis was safe. The two were reunited within hours. It had been traumatic for both of them.

As if that were not enough stress for one couple to endure, a few months later, in July 2018, the two of them were in a major car accident together. Two traumatic accidents, both involving travel, within months of one another.

At this point in the interview, Kyle told me, "You would never tell somebody before events happen that these things happen for a reason. In hindsight though, now that we've been through these horrible things, it sure is easy to ask what is it we can learn from them? And the lessons we learned were: Three hours was too long. It's too far. And life is too short."

And with that, they began looking for ways they could be together in the same city. Nelis got a new job teaching in Fort Worth, and Kyle left his church position in Austin. With nothing set in stone, Kyle said good-bye to his church family, and followed Nelis to Fort Worth. They are still in positions that are less than "permanent"—Nelis does not yet have tenure at his new job, and Kyle has taken a job as an interim minister; but they have decided on the importance of being together in the same city.

They got married in the summer of 2019, and at the time of this writing they intend to celebrate again when Nelis's family comes from South Africa. They will be celebrating in the same church where Kyle was baptized and confirmed.

I asked them at the end, What advice would you give to other couples who are facing having to move for one spouse's job?

Kyle responded: "Don't wait for the plane and the car."

Nelis agreed: "Yeah, don't wait for a sign."

But at the same time, Nelis spoke to the reality that a lot of couples are still having to make things work across distance: "What we have, even in our circle of friends, are people navigating long-distance relationships. We don't know a lot of people who are moving for one another. We know one couple where they were in Dallas together, and she just moved to Chicago for a ministry position; and he is in a specialized teaching position in Dallas, and it has been harder for him to find a job in Chicago than they had hoped."

Kyle offered this advice: "You already know that each other is the priority. So lean into that, and let the other details work themselves out."

Nelis added: "And be attentive to self-care. We both found self-care in being together, but sometimes trying to make that happen was the stressor. We would try to get on the road to see each other, but that added stress."

Kyle chimed in: "And therapy! We both had good therapists. EMDR [Eye Movement Desensitization and Reprocessing] therapy has really worked; the phantom image in my mind of the car crashing against us is more like a pencil sketch now. It's much less vivid. It went from being a blockbuster movie in my mind to being a pencil sketch—it lost the definition. So I think that helped us move along a path."

With these words of advice for couples going through difficult transitions—perhaps experiencing traumatic accidents, even—what are the lessons that seem to connect to your own family struggles? What are the sacrifices you and your family have made in navigating moves? What have been the precipitating events that led you to move? What was your discernment process like? Hopefully, by considering other ways of keeping one another in mind during the process of relocating for one family member's career, you can maintain a deeper sense of connection within and among your family members before, during, and after the move.

Creative Play: Writing Letters from Sarai

Children of pastors or military personnel are often left with no choice but to move when their parent gets a new call or stationed at a new base. Children tend to have no say in the matter. Pastor spouses and military spouses similarly can feel without a voice or say. Perhaps this text can help these family members give expression to what they are going through in this moment.

If your family is having to move or has moved, one activity that may help members process the experience is to let this story be an outlet for feelings related to moving by writing out a letter from the perspective of Sarai. If you had to imagine yourself in Sarai's shoes, leaving her homeland to follow Abram because of a call he heard from God, what might some of her inner reactions be? Take time to write out your own letter from Sarai, addressed to whomever it was that Sarai had to leave behind. Imagining what she had to say might be a way of returning voice to her, as well as to give voice to your own experiences of loss related to moving. If you have had to move to an area for a job or a family member or if you are contemplating an upcoming move, writing letters from Sarai can help give voice to what may be on your mind, and share those feelings with God.

Below, sample letters from Sarai that you could use as an example:

Dear Edith,
It's me, Sarai. We are moving on again. The countryside we are passing is like nothing I have ever seen. Each day brings with it new adventures, and fears. Did I ever tell you that I am scared of lizards? Well, each rock I sit on seems to have one waiting to jump up and scare me. It seems like every day I am being asked to trust God more and more. But it gets exhausting! I am tired of being asked to trust God, a God who promises so much—like making my husband into a great nation! Who can believe that!? And yet it is I, childless, who am expected to accompany him through all of these strange lands. So much of the burden lies on me, but can he even see it?

We are heading into Egypt soon. The food around here is become more and more scarce by the day, but we hear that Egypt still has plenty. And yet I have no idea what to make of Abram's plans for us to go and try to court favor with the pharaoh. I do not know exactly what he has up his sleeve, but he wants me to pretend that I am his sister. Ha! Yet another sacrifice I am making for him.

I get so angry sometimes, but I am powerless to express it; without Abram I would have nothing. I am out in the wilderness following him around, and if I were to stand up to him, where would that leave me? Perhaps without a husband. And that is what I need to survive out here.

But surely there is something more for me than this? Surely God has a plan for me, too, and not just for Abram? Surely God created me for a purpose!

Sometimes, I just lift my eyes to the hills and pray. "Oh, God, make your will known to me, too. Make your favor shine on me, too."

I watch and I pray, and I think of you often. Give my love to all those we have left behind.

Yours truly,
Sarai

Dear Edith,
It's me, Sarai. I have been in the court of Pharaoh. I have been one of his concubines. I have been adorned with riches I have never dreamed of. This was Abram's doing. To say I was his sister was to let Pharaoh take me as his wife. In exchange, Pharaoh has given to Abram all he could want: animals, riches, servants to wait on him. He is a rich man now. Was this what God meant by making Abram into a "great nation"!? Was this move just for his enrichment? Was it worth it? I'm afraid to ask. To Abram, I'm sure, the answer would be a definite yes. We are "better off" now than we ever have been. We have never known this much wealth. And yet . . . so much has happened between us. Can I even look at my husband again after I've been among the women of Pharaoh's house?

I feel so much sadness and anger. We risked everything for this move. We were supposed to be following God's call. But was *this* what God had in mind for me? What does God want for me here?

Pharaoh has discovered Abram's lie. After a sickness that spread through the house, Pharaoh learned that I was not Abram's sister but his wife. So we are being sent away. Not without the riches. Those we can keep. Even though I'm not sure it is worth even an ounce of what I have lost along the way.

Yours,
Sarai

These are two letters that can help give voice to some of the imagined anger and frustration and grief experienced by Sarai along the journey. Try to come up with your own letters, perhaps from the point of view of other persons who had to leave their homes—persons enslaved by Pharaoh who then had to leave Egypt with Abram when Pharaoh dismissed Abram with all that he had "acquired" while in Egypt. What can we learn from giving voice to those who were forced to follow along this move with Abram? What can these voices tell us about how we can better care for the families in our midst who are preparing to relocate or who have recently moved from another place?

Questions for Reflection

1. What whispers, silences, and missing voices are in this story of Sarai and Abram's move? And what might they say if they could speak?
2. What insights emerge from the biblical story of Sarai and Abram's move that shed light on the moves that families engage in today?
3. What lessons in this story of Sarai and Abram's move connect to your own family's struggles?
4. What are the sacrifices you and your family have made in navigating moves? What have been the precipitating events that led you to move? What was your discernment process like?
5. What can this story about Sarai and Abram's move tell us about how we can better care for the families in our midst who are preparing to relocate or who have recently moved from another place?

Chapter 5

Dealing with Infertility

Sarai and Hagar

SCRIPTURE: GENESIS 16:1–16

Introduction

It seems that almost all the important women in the Hebrew Bible struggle with infertility at some point: The matriarchs of Israel—Sarai/Sarah, Rebekah, and Rachel—as well as Samson's unnamed mother, and Hannah, the mother of the prophet Samuel, all have problems conceiving. Considering that they all give birth to very important children—or more accurately, important sons—it appears that infertility is a kind of marker that signals the impending birth of a special and remarkable male child. Infertility in the biblical text, therefore, can feel, at points, less like a real problem that these female characters face and more like a theological conundrum, easily resolved when God intercedes and miraculously "opens" these women's wombs. This vision of infertility as mainly a women's problem, which is easily fixed as soon as God intervenes— indeed, all the above named female characters overcome their infertility rather quickly after God's help—sets a rather problematic precedent for modern readers of the Bible, especially women who struggle with similar problems today, and for whom a resolution is not quickly, easily, or successfully found.

The Problem of Infertility in the Ancient Context

The portrayal of infertility as predominantly a marker of the birth of a special male child is especially problematic in that it discounts and diminishes the deep distress and fear felt by these female characters. Yet despite this imperfect focus, the feelings and emotional anguish of some of these

59

women, especially Sarai/Sarah, the focus of this chapter, still poignantly emerge from the text.

To understand Sarai's distress, we need to better understand what infertility meant in the ancient context that is reflected in the biblical text. Infertility, especially the inability to give birth to a male heir, was deeply problematic in the ancient Near East. There were significant ramifications for women who had trouble conceiving. Unable to inherit and having limited ways to make money, women were passed along as protected property from one group of men, usually fathers and sons, to another group of men, namely, her husband and her sons.

Women were therefore vulnerable and dependent on men. Without a male heir, a husband's death meant that the widow would likely end up destitute, with no one to take care of her or protect her. It is only by understanding the centrality of sons to the continued well-being of women that we can comprehend Sarai's rather desperate and befuddling decision in Genesis 16. Long unable to conceive and well past menopause (Gen. 17:17; 18:12), Sarai gives to her husband her Egyptian slave girl, Hagar, to wed and bear a male heir in her stead. In this context, the husband of an infertile woman could have taken other wives to ensure that there was a male heir. What seems unusual in this case is that Sarai takes the initiative and tries to address her own infertility by giving her husband another woman, Hagar, so that she can have a child on the family's behalf.

It is fair to say that Sarai likely would not have done this had she been able to conceive her own child. Indeed, what is illuminating about this story is how the text, without saying very much, elucidates Sarai's stress and anguish about her infertility. She must know that by giving a younger woman to her husband to bear a child that Hagar's status in the family might be elevated. Sarai thus risks her own standing as the head female of this family with her decision. She might even be risking more than just her status. What if Abram decides Sarai is useless to him and throws her out? That she is willing to undertake such risks in order to obtain a male heir shows her utter desperation; and in so doing, it allows us a glimpse, albeit silent, into the distress, sadness, fear, and desperation that infertile women like Sarai feel.

In contrast to Sarai's desperate actions, Abram is frustratingly passive and silent. And his passivity elucidates how differently childlessness affected men in this context. Though Abram is also worried about the lack of a male heir—indeed, he asks God directly about this problem at points (Gen. 15:1–6; 17:17–19)—as a patriarch, he is not nearly as frantic as Sarai is. Indeed, when Sarai explains to Abram that God has prevented her from conceiving and that therefore Abram should take Hagar as a surrogate, Abram willingly assents but says nothing (16:2). It is not difficult to see that Sarai proposes this plan because of her distress. That Abram asks his wife nothing about it, however, is disturbing and disappointing. Why doesn't he ask Sarai about what she is going through and whether she is comfortable with what she is proposing? Why doesn't he try to figure out another way forward?

To be fair to Abram, he might not be as anguished or distressed about Sarah's infertility because he himself had received assurances from God that his descendants will be numerous. Considering that the mother of these children has not yet been specified, perhaps Abram goes along willingly with Sarai's plan because he thinks that this is God's plan coming into fruition. Certainly, the fact that Sarai's plan entails sexual relations with a younger woman might play a part in Abram's quick and silent assent.

Yet the lack of communication here is still rather troubling. We have observed that Abram seems unconcerned and silent. We will also notice that God is distressingly reticent in this passage as well. For while Abram has so far received direct assurances from God that he will be a progenitor of innumerable descendants, at no point does God reassure Sarai, who seems upset and desperate about her infertility. Indeed, it might even be the case that Sarai has been told about God's promises to her husband and is trying to help fulfill God's plan by putting its fruition above her own needs and desires. If so, then why doesn't God tell Sarai that she is wrong—that there is no need to get Hagar involved because Sarai herself will soon bear this desired male heir? Why doesn't God say something, anything to the desperate matriarch, instead of waiting until Genesis 18 to talk to her indirectly?

This lack of divine communication is especially problematic considering that Sarai thinks, as was believed in the ancient context, that infertility is something that stems from God. Indeed, as she tells Abram, ". . . the LORD has prevented me from bearing . . ." (16:2). As evident by this statement, she seems to believe that infertility is a kind of theological problem for which she is to blame. If God is in charge of fertility, and if male children are central to the success of a family, then she must have offended God somehow to be unable to conceive. Again, God's silence is befuddling. Why doesn't God assure Sarai that she has done nothing wrong? That her continued infertility is not because of any fault on her part but because of the particularities of God's plan? Why doesn't God assure Sarai, as he does with Abram, that she will indeed conceive soon—that she too alongside Abram will be a progenitor of a great nation and innumerable descendants?

Going from ancient text to the modern world, Sarai's self-blame reflects similar feelings that infertile women might feel today. Infertility is still largely seen as a woman's problem, and it is still usually women who are subtly blamed for infertility: Perhaps she had the wrong priorities and waited too long to have a child; perhaps she has a bad diet or is not healthy enough; maybe she is exercising too much or too little; or perhaps this is all part of God's unknowable plan for this woman.

Compounding the problem, biblical stories about infertility can make women who are currently struggling with infertility feel worse, not better. Many of these stories follow a particular sequence: A female character is distressed by her infertility; God, sometimes as a result of prayer and sometimes without explanation, decides to open the character's womb; and the woman magically and quickly conceives and gives birth to a divinely ordained son. This sequence of events, because they are found in stories in the Bible, can lead to misguided theological expectations and assumptions. Namely, that women who are struggling with infertility can simply overcome this problem with enough faith; that if someone is faithful enough, God will surely open her womb as God did with Sarai, Rebekah, Rachel, and Hannah.[1] This in turn compounds the blame and sense of guilt.

There are still other troubling messages that emerge from this story about Sarai's infertility. Though never fully spelled out, perhaps Sarai believes that Hagar will act as a kind of surrogate to a son who will perhaps be turned over to Sarai and be adopted as her own. Or perhaps Sarai has convinced herself that what is really important is that the family has a male heir, and suppresses her discomfort with the situation. Whatever the case, things do not go according to plan. Hagar, conceiving rather quickly—which again plays on the stereotype of the over-fertile Egyptians that we saw in the last chapter (cf. Gen. 12:10–20)—realizes that she is no longer a slave but now the bearer of Abram's child. As such, she recognizes that her status has been elevated in the family and acts accordingly. It states that when Hagar realizes she has so easily conceived, that Sarai, her mistress, was belittled or lowered in her eyes (16:4). Sarai, angry with this sudden change in status, confronts Abram who, oddly passive, allows Sarai to mistreat Hagar so badly that Hagar runs away (16:6).

Despite there being a putatively satisfactory conclusion to this story—an angel of the Lord finds Hagar and convinces her to go back home and submit to her mistress (16:9)—the first family of Israel is hardly a shining example of domestic tranquility. The bulk of the criticism has landed on the two women, both of whom seem to be subtly criticized by the text and whom are in essence pitted against each other. Sarai, who is in a position of higher status than Hagar, gives Hagar to her husband as if she is mere property and then mistreats Hagar when she conceives. Remember that Hagar, as a foreign slave woman, has no rights and no say as to whether she in essence will be raped by Abram and made to bear his child.

Hagar's situation and her powerlessness cannot but remind readers of similar situations in the history of the United States and in other countries around the world. When slavery was legal in the United States, female slaves were raped and impregnated without say by their white owners, sometimes with full knowledge of these men's wives. Hagar, like so many who are marginalized or powerless, be it because of their gender, class, age, or ethnicity, is exploited and abused by those who are more powerful. Indeed, in a world where sex trafficking, exploitation, and slavery are still present, modern-day Hagars abound.

Yet the text is not wholly sympathetic to Hagar's lot either. As soon as she realizes that she is pregnant, she seems to gloat in her easy ability to conceive in front of a woman who has issues with infertility and who likely feels rather badly about this. Indeed, the portrayals of both women are patriarchal and biased. This story pits one woman against another, lumping them into easy binary categories of fertile versus infertile, rich versus poor, ethnic insider versus outsider. Yet despite this text's obvious sexism, this story reveals the inequities, stresses, trauma, and pressures that are experienced by women in a patriarchal context in which they are deprived of their rights and authority. In a misogynistic context, women are compelled to fight against each other instead of helping each other. Indeed, division is part of the ploy by which the powerful remain in power.

Indeed, if we read against the text, and interrogate the patriarchal tendencies that undergird this story, we find that the male characters are even more problematically portrayed than their female counterparts. Abram's passivity and lack of feeling, both for his wife Sarai who is beset with problems and anguish, as well as toward Hagar whom Abram allows to be mistreated despite her being pregnant with his child, is horrifying. As evident, if Abram is indeed the "master" of his household, then he is a very bad manager, because his household is in complete disarray. Along with Abram, God, who in the Hebrew Bible is usually presented as a male deity, also comes off rather badly. As noted above, God never talks to or reassures Sarai despite her distress, and though God does send an angel to help the fleeing Hagar—indeed, Hagar is the first woman in the Bible whom God talks to with an angel as the messenger—ultimately the angel tells Hagar to return and to submit to her mistress's abuse. If this is God, why doesn't God simply rescue Hagar and set her up someplace safe? As in previous episodes, we are forced to confront the deficiencies of a supposedly perfect being. It is difficult to look up to and perhaps even have much faith in a deity that tells a fleeing slave woman who has been raped by her male owner and abused by her female owner to return and submit.

As an advertisement for God and his patriarch, therefore, this tale is certainly lacking. As a tale that confronts the problems and ugliness that accompany certain aspects of many relationships, however, it has much to offer. Indeed, there are several positive effects of this story. First, it elucidates the stresses, the self-blame, pressures, and insensitivity that women who struggle with infertility deal with; in so doing, this story shows the need for church leaders and people of faith to realize that women who struggle with infertility also struggle theologically as well. This is especially the case in the church because these biblical miracle stories send the message that infertility can simply be overcome with faith. Indeed, not just theology, but this tale also shows that infertility and fertility is bound up with issues of gender, race, class, religion, and power. Thus this narrative points to the ways in which patriarchy, misogyny, and sexism undergird a system that harms, abuses, and exploits women, children, and the powerless. And in so doing, it encourages us to think more deeply and to interrogate stories and organizations that we deem sacred, such as the church, in order to expose such abuses.

Families Facing Infertility Today

What do the experiences of the women facing infertility in the book of Genesis tell us about families today who are trying to have a child? The word "infertility" can be part of the problem, in that it takes us a step away from the experience of what these families are going through. It is a clinical term, and the word does not do justice to the pain that these families feel.

Other words or phrases might come closer to the experience, such as: secret suffering, monthly dreams dashed, and intimacy exchanged for doctors' cold hands. The phrase "secret suffering" describes infertility because women who are trying to have children do not tell the world each time they find out they are not pregnant. Each time the pregnancy test comes back negative, or the in vitro fertilization (IVF) treatment fails, there is no community to share this with; it feels too private and too painful to bring before a Sunday school class or with coworkers around a water cooler. "Monthly dreams dashed" means that every cycle where a woman ovulates becomes an opportunity to hope for pregnancy, and every month that woman's hopes are raised, and when her period starts again those dreams literally go down the drain. "Intimacy exchanged for doctors' cold hands" refers to the fact that a woman seeking treatment for infertility has to go through a number of tests where doctors evaluate all of her "private" parts, and through the process she and her partner have to give up their own ideas of intimacy as they share personal details and give samples of bodily fluids with medical personnel. The lovemaking the couple had hoped would bring them a child is no longer the central focus: Now, they must rely on doctors and nurses and microscopic tools to make the miracle of life take place. And even then, there is no guarantee. Doctors cannot guarantee a baby to a couple, and there are many who go through multiple rounds of fertility treatment—and thousands of dollars—only to end up right back where they started: still without a baby.

I asked a good friend, Jen, to share with me her experiences for this book. Jen is a teacher and math specialist, helping teachers educate their students. Her husband, Bri, is a high school counselor. Individually, they are each some of the most wonderful people you will ever meet. Together, they are one amazing couple, each bringing out the best in the other. They also struggled for three years to have children. Jen told me that looking back over her journals from that time period, she remembers that each month, each time she thought she might be pregnant, she went into planning mode. She would think, "OK, so the baby would be born at this time of year, which means she or he would start kindergarten in that particular year, etc." Each time she learned she was not pregnant felt like the loss of a dream, the loss of a life: a type of miscarriage. Month after month after month. She said, "We don't really talk about miscarriage in the church. But each time I learned I was not pregnant after thinking that I was, each time felt like I had miscarried. And all those dreams, then, had to die. All those plans I had already made for that particular baby."

After exhausting other fertility treatments and options, Jen and Bri went through IVF to try and conceive. She explained how her own body felt numb, being looked at and inspected and examined by so many doctors and nurses. She said, "It felt totally out of our control. Bri had to do his business in a cup, they took the sperm and examined it under a microscope, cut off the tail and injected it into one of my eggs, and then put it back into my body." She said it felt like they were relying entirely on these doctors to put a baby in her body.

Jen and Bri are among the lucky ones. Their IVF treatments led to the birth of two healthy baby boys, now five and four. With the fog of parenting young children, Jen said it is hard for her to remember everything from their years of trying to conceive, but she still remembers them as painful.

I asked her if all of those times she spent planning and dreaming for the baby she thought she had conceived actually prepared her in any way for the children she has now.

"Absolutely not," she answered. "All those plans and the foiling of those dreams were like the water that softened my rough edges. Children require a lack of plans because they have their own plans. It was a wearing-down process for me, a training for *not* having plans. We are not in control. My children have taught me that they have their own timing and their own plans, and I have learned to give up my own need to control."

Especially during those months when they were trying to conceive, she said, letting go of control and trying to stay present was really hard: "This process required me to be in the present because you cannot plan for the future. Every month you don't get pregnant and have to go again. . . . Being present in those years was really hard."

I asked her if during the time she and Bri were trying to conceive, if any of the biblical stories were any comfort. She thought about it, and responded, "I don't know—maybe they were able to live more in the present than I was. To be honest, I'd have to say no, the Bible didn't offer me any comfort at the time. But what was comforting were the people who had actually gone through this experience: coworkers, friends, people at church. And so if anything, if the church can be a place where these things get talked about more, if more couples could share their experiences with one another, then I think that would be really helpful."

Jen now knows many couples who have gone through infertility treatment. In fact, she says, "We know almost no one who was just able to have a baby without some help." The prevalence of couples struggling to conceive and the number of couples currently undergoing various forms of fertility treatment suggests that the church needs to be a place where we can talk more openly about this experience and be able to bring our complaints and concerns before a God who is in all these struggles with us.

We may not be able to fully understand what it was like for the women in the Bible to have to wait on God for a child, but perhaps their experiences can be a jumping-off point where we can share our experiences today. By letting these women's experiences be the focus of a sermon or a small group study, perhaps more couples will be able to share in the sense that they are not alone, that others around them have already gone through this, and they can find comfort in the company.

There are still childless couples whose stories do not end the way that Jen and Bri's did. There are couples who went through IVF only to have each treatment end in miscarriage. There are couples who go through this process, only to go through an entire nine months of pregnancy and lose the baby at the very end. It is difficult to talk about these painful experiences; but if we cannot talk about them in the places that should bring us closer to God, where will we find comfort? How can churches do better in their ministries to all people, not focusing only on families with children but also on couples and persons who are single? Can the church help all persons feel included in the family of the church, whether or not they have children or spouses? Hopefully, starting these conversations in your congregation can begin to open up avenues for more and more members to feel fully embraced and included.

Another story Jen shared stood out to me. She said that now, every time she is in a space where someone announces that they are pregnant, she looks around the room "to see who else might be holding back tears." Jen reflected on how hard Mother's Day can be for so many women, those who cannot be mothers or who are trying to be mothers or who have lost children: "Motherhood is a really sensitive issue."

In light of motherhood being a sensitive issue, how can churches reimagine that day known as "Mother's Day," which is celebrated in May? Some churches have reworded it to be "Woman's Day" to focus less on the experiences of motherhood. It can also be a time to name some of the pain and loss women experience around motherhood. What about using this day as an opportunity to educate the congregation about the experiences couples may be facing?

Jen directed me to one resource she found helpful for naming ways friends and family could support couples facing infertility: an organization called RESOLVE, available online through the National Infertility Association (https://resolve.org/support/for-friends-and-family/). Their website points out that couples dealing with infertility will eventually "resolve the infertility problem in one of three ways: they will eventually conceive a baby; they will stop the infertility treatments and choose to live without children; they will find an alternative way to parent, such as by adopting a child or becoming a foster parent. Reaching a resolution can take years." In the meantime, couples who are wanting to conceive need emotional support from their family and friends.

Sometimes, well-intended friends and family, trying to be supportive, can inadvertently say the wrong thing. Suggesting to a childless couple that they must have a lot more free time on their hands, or some other way of trying to make their situation seem better because of living childfree, is not a helpful way of offering support to these couples. The RESOLVE website gives a list of things for people *not* to say to couples struggling with infertility, including: "Don't tell them to relax. Don't minimize the problem. Don't say there are worse things that could happen. Don't say they aren't meant to be parents. Don't ask why they aren't trying IVF. Don't be crude. Don't complain about your pregnancy. Don't push adoption (yet). Let them know that you care. Support their decision to stop treatments."[2]

There are also couples who make the conscious decision to *not* have children, and who have not experienced infertility or gone through infertility treatments. So another thing to watch out for is assuming that childless couples are somehow missing out on parenting or that they must be struggling with infertility because they do not have children. It is never a good idea to ask a couple about their "plans" for having children; as we have heard from parents like Jen, infertility destroys any such plans, and besides that, there are couples who plan to never become parents, and it is important to respect their decision.

In addition to educating the church about the etiquette around infertility, other ways the church can support couples include offering other ways for adults to be part of the life of children. In an interview with Margaret Aymer, a professor of New Testament and also adoptive mother, she shared with me that our society looks with suspicion on childless couples who want to interact with other people's children. She and her husband were childless for eight years before their son was born to his birth parents, and during that time, she was surrounded by women who were overburdened with the task of parenting, and yet who couldn't ask the childless couple for help because "what would we want with their kids?" People who do not have children may also be great teachers and nursery caregivers, and yet are we afraid to ask childless people to fill those roles in our churches? There are many wonderful men and women serving in places where they regularly interact with children: in schools, as teachers and social workers and counselors, and we do not require that they be parents themselves in order to fill these positions. Why should we expect people who volunteer in our churches to be parents? It may or may not be something that a person or couple would like to do, but we should offer them the opportunity, just as we would invite parents to serve in children's ministry roles.

Finally, another way to support couples could be through services of healing and wholeness. There are "Longest Night" services that some churches hold around Christmas to pray for persons who are sick or in need of prayer, who have lost loved ones in the past year, or who are feeling especially challenged by the expectations around the holiday season. Other churches may offer prayer services on a monthly basis. These would be excellent opportunities to include mention of miscarriages as a grief experienced by persons present in the congregation. The "long night" of waiting and grief can be named and lifted up before God.

In the prayers of the people that take place on a weekly basis in worship could be another time to mention praying for couples who are struggling with infertility, letting them know they are being remembered and kept in mind by others in the congregation and by God. If preachers could lift up the experiences in their sermons and name the silent pain of miscarriage, they could set an example for others in the congregation for how to support one another. In small groups, as couples get to know others and share their experiences with miscarriage and infertility, naming those losses in prayer with and for one another can also be an important source of support.

Each child born is a miracle. Whether conceived by what my friend Jen calls the "home method" or through medical fertility support, each child born is a miracle. Each step in the process is risky, each step is riddled with fear of loss, and parents who have lost children can tell you: nothing is guaranteed. For this reason, it is important that we focus on supporting couples throughout the process.

While there have been questions about the ethics of IVF, with critics concerned about what happens to fertilized embryos that are not implanted, and warning us of "designer babies" chosen for their genetic makeup, these questions tend to look judgmentally on people who go through IVF, rather than consider their experiences of suffering. The kind of suffering that leads to people paying thousands of dollars for IVF includes the heartbreak of infertility as well as the awareness of genetic diseases passed on through the generations. For those people who want to protect their children from having to worry about these particular diseases affecting them in the future, there is no illusion that their child will be "designer" in any way except for not having the particular gene that would otherwise have led to a terrible disease. Having a child who is free of one particular disease, on the other hand, does not guarantee that the child will not be afflicted by another particular disease. There are no genetic markers for a host of illnesses and diseases that can radically impact a person's life. There are no genetic predictors for car accidents or other ways harm can befall us. Focusing on the "ethics" of IVF and questioning these decisions will not get us closer to alleviating human suffering. But supporting people who are having to make difficult decisions brings us closer as a human family.

God uses medicine to heal us; people with diabetes or heart disease can testify to the impact of medicine on managing their symptoms and helping them live lives more fully. Why then would we place limits on God's ability to work through medicine to bring us the gift of new life? The families in the Hebrew Bible/Old Testament did not have the advantage of medical advances that we have today. And yet just as we can imagine Sarai feeling left out of the process of conceiving a child in her old age—feeling the situation to be out of her control—the same feelings of being out of control of the process also accompanies couples who are pursuing IVF and fertility treatments today. They do not know the outcome. They are not assured or guaranteed a baby at the end. We need to be able to trust couples struggling with infertility to make the best decisions they can under the circumstances and to support them throughout the process. If we believe in a relational God who supports us and accompanies us throughout life, then we need to live that out in how we accompany one another through the struggles we face. God works through us in comforting and providing support to one another, and our loving support with and for one another knits us together as a human family.

Questions for Reflection

1. How does it feel to read the story of Abram and Sarai and Hagar in this way, opening the story to critique and questioning? Does it help you see them as people with imperfections and struggles who God also was able to work through?
2. How does it feel to question how God is presented in the story? Is it stressful to think about challenging the portrayal of God in the Bible? Are you able to see your relationship with God as separate from your relationship to the Bible?
3. Have you struggled with trying to conceive a child, or do you know someone who has? What resonated with you from Jen and Bri's story of trying to conceive?

4. What are some of the ways you have changed over time in how you have thought about what it means to be a family? What are the messages you have heard from society about what family means? What are the messages the church sends about what counts as family?
5. What do you believe now about what it means to be a human family? What are some ways you can actively help others feel part of the human family? Where do you see God at work bringing the human family together?

Chapter 6

Blended Families

Abraham, Sarah, Hagar, and Ishmael

SCRIPTURE: GENESIS 21:1–21

Introduction

"One big happy family." How many times have we heard this phrase used to describe an ideal that falls far short of any reality we know in our own families? Hopefully, there are instances in each of our lives when we do experience our family as a happy place. Yet to talk of "one big happy family," we are typically using the expression tongue-in-cheek, with a bit of sarcasm. The truth is, often families are not happy, and large groups of people rarely get along perfectly. There is conflict in every organization and institution, even those that pride themselves on being like "one big happy family." In this chapter, we will be peeling back some of the layers behind the facade of "one big happy family," relaying some of the more painful interactions among key figures in our biblical narrative. Along the way we will hear resonances of the struggles that families experience in trying to bring together different people to form a family, and we will look at the end at how modern families are trying to navigate these spaces of different forms of blended families.

Blended Families in the Bible

Sarah and Abraham are known as the first matriarch and patriarch of Israel, and therefore accorded much respect and renown. They are the parents of Isaac, and through Isaac, the line of descendants chosen or elected by God known as the Israelites. However, what is usually forgotten is that Sarah, whose name was previously Sarai, and Abraham, previously Abram, are not the only members of this immediate family.

73

Rather, there are two other members: Hagar, Abraham's second wife and the former slave woman of Sarah, and Hagar's child, Ishmael. Their family, in other words, is a blended family—different, certainly, from the blended families we have today as polygamy is no longer widely accepted in the West—but a blended family nonetheless. As a result, reflected in the story of this family are some of the same challenges and problems that blended families faced in the past, and which they continue to face in the present. Like so many stories from the Bible, the tale of this blended family does not offer solutions so much as an empathetic and very human glimpse into the complex nature of familial relationships.

Hagar as Sarah's Surrogate and Rival

As discussed in the previous chapter on infertility, Hagar's story begins in Genesis 16 when she is given by her mistress, Sarah, to Abraham to be his second wife so that she can conceive a male heir that Sarah is too old to bear. This leads, predictably, to antagonism and a breakdown of the relationship between the two women, and Sarah mistreats Hagar so badly that she runs away (Gen. 16:6). Hagar is found by an angel of the Lord who persuades her to return and submit to Sarah, and who tells her that she will bear a son who will also become an ancestor of many descendants (Gen. 16:10). As was noted in the preceding chapter, this first story of Hagar's flight—of which there are two such stories—offers problematic portrayals of female characters, especially those struggling with infertility and also those who are in a position of powerlessness. It also paints Abraham and God in an equally if not more troubling manner.

Especially questionable is God's failure to communicate to Sarah that her infertility is a temporary situation. More important, God also seems to have forgotten to tell all the parties involved—Hagar, Sarah, and Abraham—that the identity of the mother matters in terms of which male child will inherit God's promises to Abraham and therefore become God's chosen or elect. Indeed, it is only after Hagar gets pregnant, flees, and then returns that God decides to tell Abraham directly and Sarah indirectly that Sarah, despite her age, will conceive a son (Gen. 18:9–10); and that it will be this son and not the son of Hagar who will become God's elect and bearer of the Abrahamic promise (Gen. 17:19). The Abrahamic promise entailed a covenant or an agreement promising a special relationship with this deity as well as land and progeny. The uncommunicative portrayal of God is puzzling and adds to the family drama and tension. Why doesn't God say to Abraham or Sarah that there is no need for this complicated family situation because Hagar's child is ultimately not going to be chosen by God?

God's silence seems to hint that the birth of Ishmael, despite Ishmael not becoming the chosen heir to the Abrahamic promise—at least not in Judaism and Christianity—was part of God's plan all along. If so, bespeaking their importance, God's plan might entail the promulgation of such blended families. Indeed, the significance of a blended family, especially the presence and birth of Ishmael, the son who is not chosen though still envisioned in the text as cared for and important to God (Gen. 17:20; 21:18), highlights a particular theological conundrum that stems from the idea of election. Divine election or chosenness, the idea on which the history of Israel is centered, is theologically problematic in that it feels and looks like divine favoritism.

Now divine favoritism, though it sounds bad, is only problematic in certain situations. This favoritism is not a problem if Israel's god is imagined as a kind of family or local deity. Just as you might like or care more about your friends or family or people in your own town, so a local or family deity would obviously be most interested in those that they considered their own. However, when a particular deity goes from being local or regional god, with a small letter g, to God, with a capital G, then divine favoritism becomes more problematic. That is, divine favoritism seems unfair when there is only *one* universal deity who is supposed to be everyone's God. With a universal deity, divine favoritism suddenly looks like inequality and injustice.

The story about God's interest and care of Ishmael and of the blended family might be an attempt to partially resolve this theological problem of election. God's care of Ishmael shows that God cares for everyone, even those who are not chosen or who are unelect. Not being chosen does not mean being rejected by God. As such, this God is the God of everyone. God, while caring for the unelect, is still particularly concerned with the child of Sarah who will go on to be the elect descendant chosen to fulfill God's promises to Abraham. And in this, divine favoritism is not wholly absent in this tale either. In short, this story recognizes and perhaps even wants to legitimize divine favoritism while at the same time expressing some discomfort with this idea, probably because divine favoritism and the universalism of God (that God is the God of everyone) don't really fit together very well.

As we saw with Cain and Abel, and later with Jacob and Esau, the biblical text will continue to struggle with this idea of divine favoritism throughout the corpus; and in so doing, it is really wrestling with the problem of unfairness. While we might wish for a world that is ruled and controlled by one fair God who loves everyone equally, we recognize this is not the world that we know and live in. In our world, some of us are luckier—born richer, in a better place, with better parents, with more beauty or intelligence or gifts than others. As such, we reside in a world where some mode of divine favoritism or random luck seems to be present. Indeed, if we think about it a bit deeper, this desire for a wholly fair world and a wholly fair God might not be universal. Many of us, though we don't like to admit it, actually want a God that likes us or our family just a little bit more, a God who is on our side and who is willing to tip the scale in our favor; in other words, a God who has chosen us, who prefers us. The biblical text in struggling with election evinces the same struggle between what the world looks like and what we want it to be; between our desire for fairness and our desire for preferential treatment. Written by the scribes who claimed descent from Sarah, the text declares that, in this blended family, God likely liked Sarah's child, and therefore Sarah's descendants, a bit better than the child (and the descendants) of Hagar.

Conflict, Division and Separation of the Blended Family

Related to divine favoritism is the closely associated phenomenon of parental favoritism and divided allegiances and loyalties—issues that are still likely present in and struggled over in blended families. Indeed, the blended family of Hagar and Sarah reflect similar concerns. By Genesis 21:2, Sarah finally conceives and bears a son, whom Abraham names Isaac, which means "to laugh" or "to play." Like so many etiologies and etymologies of names in the Hebrew Bible, Isaac's name is explained multiple times. In Genesis 18:9–15, Isaac's name is explained as a result of Sarah who laughs, likely out of incredulity and disbelief, when she overhears God telling Abraham that she will soon bear a child in her old age. Isaac's name is explained again in Genesis 21:6 after he is born. Here, Isaac is named Isaac because his mother, Sarah, is so joyous when she finally gives birth that she states that God has made laughter for her. She states furthermore that anyone who hears about the miraculous birth of Isaac will also laugh, either out of disbelief or out of delight over her situation.

Isaac's birth and, as we will soon see, the meaning of his name will have significant effects on the relationships among his family members in this blended family. Notably, the relationship between the two wives—Hagar and Sarah—becomes even more tense after Sarah gives birth to her own son. Things come to head during the party for Isaac's weaning. In the ancient context, when infants frequently died, weaning indicated that the child would likely survive. Hence, Isaac's weaning party is celebration of and likely an acknowledgment that he would live on.

What this meant for this blended family, however, was that there were now two possible heirs to Abraham's fortune and also to the promises given to him by God. That Isaac would be the bearer of the Abrahamic promise is made clear by the authors of the text early on in Genesis 21 as they subtly note that Isaac, unlike Ishmael, was born of the right mother and was circumcised at the right time, that is, on the eighth day (Gen. 21:4). Ishmael, in contrast, is circumcised when he is thirteen years old, as we find out in Genesis 17:25. As I noted earlier, election is similar to divine favoritism. And if you read the account of Israel's first families in Genesis, God has a tendency to favor second- or younger-born sons and to choose them as the bearer of the divine promise. Indeed, both Isaac and his son and elect heir, Jacob, are second-born sons.

Another way to think about God's favoritism of second-born sons is that God seems to prefer underdogs. Second-born sons in the ancient context usually did not inherit as much of the wealth as the firstborn and did not serve as the heirs that carried on the family's legacy. Hence, God's favoritism is ambivalent. On the one hand, God does not seem to like everyone equally in the Bible. On the other hand, God seems to prefer the unlikely, the underdog—or according to liberation theology, the poor and the marginalized. The seeming unfairness of God's favoritism is balanced out by the divine preference for the marginalized and the weak.

While God favors the second-born or the underdog, human society, however, especially in the ancient context, very much favored the firstborn son. It was this son who was the male heir, and it was this son who would inherit double the portion of the family's wealth. Hence, when Isaac is born, the identity of the son who would become the inheritor of the material resources of the family becomes more confusing and contested. Usually in this context, the firstborn son—that is, Ishmael—would have been the recipient of the double share of the inheritance. Sarah, cognizant of this fact, works quickly to make sure that it is her son—and not that of the other wife—who will inherit majority stakes. This conflict and the monetary roots of it might reflect similar situations and problems that the modern blended family deals with. Who gets what money and what material benefits, what is deemed fair, and who should pay for what are fraught but necessary questions that need to be worked out, especially in blended families where multiple parents and children are involved. Related to the issue of money are concerns about parental favoritism and issues of loyalty, especially in modern blended families. Unlike in the biblical story in which Sarah favors her own biological child, and indeed, as we will see, works to force out the other wife and her stepson, in modern situations loyalties and favoritism might be less centered on biological relationships. Indeed, loyalties and favoritism might shift and change as time goes on.

In the case of Sarah and Hagar, after the birth of Isaac, Sarah, who fears for the inheritance of her biological son, Isaac, moves quickly to push her rival and her rival's son out of the household. This is the second story about Hagar's expulsion in the Bible. Earlier, in Genesis 16, Hagar runs away while she is pregnant because of Sarah's mistreatment, only to be told to return to Abraham and Sarah's house by an angel. Here the separation is more permanent and the reasons for it are murkier. During the party for Isaac's weaning—notice that there was no such party for Ishmael and Hagar—Sarah sees something so disturbing (Gen. 21:9) that she forces Abraham, who again is rather passive, to expel Hagar and Ishmael from the family's home (21:10). This expulsion into the desert with only a skin of water meant certain death for Hagar and Ishmael. What is it that Sarah sees, and what can possibly, if anything, justify Sarah's harsh reaction? Indeed, the only way that the readers can judge and evaluate Sarah's action, whether she acted correctly or overreacted, is to know and understand what she sees at the party.

The problem is that the text is not really clear as to what Sarah sees Ishmael doing (and here, I would recommend that the reader compare several translations of Gen. 21:9). In Genesis 21:9, the Hebrew text states that Sarah saw Ishmael "isaacing" her son, Isaac. The verb here is ambiguous in meaning, but it is clear that this verb is related to the word and name of Isaac. As I noted earlier, Isaac's name can mean to laugh or even to play. Indeed, some interpreters have argued that Isaac, reflecting his name, is a rather funny or humorous character.[1] If so, then what Sarah sees perhaps is Ishmael joking around or simply playing with his half brother. Or perhaps, it is much more aggressive. Maybe Sarah sees Ishmael laughing at her son or making fun of him or joking around at his expense. Notice how if it is the first scenario—Ishmael is joking with his brother and just having a good time at the party—Sarah overreacts and merely uses Ishmael's actions as an excuse to get her rival and the other child removed from the house. Sarah's actions are easier to comprehend, though still rather harsh, if what she sees is a second possible scenario: Ishmael mocking or laughing at Isaac.

Her actions are even more understandable if we consider a third definition of the verb, "isaacing." As noted earlier, this verb sounds like Issac's
name. Perhaps then what Sarah sees is Ishmael imitating Isaac or acting
like Isaac, that is, acting like the chosen heir. Seeing Ishmael acting like
Isaac reminds Sarah that her son has a competitor; and perhaps this is why
she forces Abraham to throw out Hagar and Ishmael. Though Sarah still
acts rather harshly, perhaps she is triggered by seeing Ishmael imitating
Isaac. After all, God never tells Sarah directly—only Abraham—that it is
her son who will inherit the Abrahamic promise; and hence, Sarah has
reason to worry and perhaps a reason to try to push out her son's rival.

Sarah's actions, however, are much more justified if she witnesses a
possible fourth scenario. This verb that describes what Ishmael is doing
to Isaac is used infrequently in the biblical text. One of the few times it is
used is in Genesis 26:8. In Genesis 26, the grown-up Isaac, like his father,
Abraham, ends up in another country where he has to lie that his wife
is his sister so as to remain safe. Unlike with Abraham, however, Isaac's
lie is discovered because he acts foolishly: The leader of that country
looks out the window and sees Isaac "isaacing" his wife, Rebekah, and
realizes that they are not siblings but husband and wife (Gen. 26:8–9). As
evident, the verb in this instance seems to connote something sexual. If
so, then Ishmael's "isaacing" of Isaac—the act that Sarah witnesses—is
much more disturbing and hints of abuse in the family. According to
this meaning of the verb, the text hints that what Sarah sees that makes
her so angry is Ishmael doing something sexual and, hence, abusive to
Isaac who is just a baby. If so, then Sarah's actions become much more
justifiable and understandable. She is merely defending her child from
an abusive sibling.

The problem with all these interpretations, however, is that the text
is unclear. The biblical writers deliberately use an ambiguous verb to
describe Ishmael's action, and in so doing, they leave the interpretation
and the judgment of Sarah's actions and, hence, Ishmael's innocence for
the reader to decide.

Even if Sarah's actions were understandable, however, it is difficult not
to feel for this family and especially for Hagar, who is the clearest victim in this tale. Hagar does nothing wrong. Rather, everything is done
to her without her okay or her say. Given first to a woman as a slave,
she is then given to her mistress's husband to be sexually taken advantage
of, conceives his son, is mistreated so much that she is compelled to run
away, only to be told to return and submit. After all of this, she is again
expelled into the desert with only limited water and food because her son

might have done something to upset Sarah. And all this is OK'd by God in Genesis 21:12 who again tells Abraham to listen to his wife Sarah and to succumb to her demands. The saving grace is that God does not abandon Hagar and Ishmael to die in the wilderness but instead helps her find water and is said to have been with Ishmael as he grew up (Gen. 21:17–21).

Understandably, African American readers and communities have resonated with Hagar's story. Hagar, we must recall, is an Egyptian slave woman, and unlike in the modern context, ancient Egypt, at points, encompassed parts of northern Africa. As such, her story gives hope that the God who twice rescued the slave woman, Hagar, and twice promised her that her descendants will not only live but thrive—that this God will similarly uplift communities made up of modern-day Hagars and Ishmaels.

The discord in this blended family, which culminates with the expulsion of Hagar and Ishmael, will have a lingering effect. Within the context of the biblical story, there will be comeuppance for Sarah's mistreatment of Hagar. Later in the book of Exodus, Hagar's descendants, coming full circle, will mistreat and enslave the descendants of Sarah until God again comes to their rescue by sending a leader, Moses.

Though this story about the family of Sarah, Hagar, and Abraham is about the discord and eventual fracturing of this blended family, it does not, however, fully extinguish the hope that such a family can eventually work through their issues and become stronger as a result. Indeed, bespeaking a possible reconciliation, we are told in Genesis 25:9 that both Ishmael and Isaac reunited to bury their father, Abraham. Despite the tension in the family, the two brothers seem to have partially amended their relationship in the future. Indeed, as we will see in later chapters, Ishmael and Isaac are not the only siblings in the biblical text who will reconcile and heal, to some degree, their familial wounds.

Blended Families Today

Once again, we read an example of a family story that does not give us a clear "how to" in terms of guiding us how to relate to one another today. The mistreatment of Hagar and the casting off of Abraham and Hagar's son, Ishmael, is not a story that lifts up values that blended families today would want to copy. The story is tragic. But again, returning to the idea that we can read the Bible relationally and distinguish our relationship with the Bible from our relationship with God, perhaps we can find in this story a mirror of human suffering today and the whispers of God's care for families divided in the present.

Thinking about the story of this biblical blended family, there are several ways we can reflect on the theme of blended families. By thinking about the ways oppressed communities have identified with these characters—such as African American biblical scholars identifying with Hagar's experiences—we can consider ongoing challenges for our human family in addressing the painful legacy of racism. By considering the way Ishmael has served as a pivotal figure for Muslims, we can consider how our larger human family is a blend of religious traditions. Finally, we can consider actual blended families today and how they can be successfully incorporating people into their family who are not related to them by blood.

Hagar and the Experiences of Black Women

Delores Williams, an African American theologian, wrote a book titled *Sisters in the Wilderness: The Challenge of Womanist God-Talk*. Williams reads the biblical story of Hagar and compares it to the experiences of enslaved Black women who were forced to bear children for their slave masters.[2] In addition to forced surrogacy, enslaved Black women often had to take care of the master's white children, a role that continued after slavery's end often due to economic hardship and other societal pressures. Black women had to take on this nurturing role for white children, often at the expense of the nurturance of their own children.

And yet, for Williams, the story of Hagar is also an image of resilience and strength. Though she had to endure being forced to bear a child for Abraham and then suffering the abuse from her slave mistress, Sarah, Hagar took the risk of fleeing (Gen. 16). In the second flight narrative (Gen. 21), Hagar and Ishmael are free but wandering in the wilderness. This experience, says Williams, mirrors the suffering of Black families, trying to survive in the economic and political wilderness of constant discrimination long after slavery's end, continuing on to the present.[3] Williams points to segregation and systemic racism as the ongoing wilderness Black families are forced into, with Black children still at risk of losing their lives, just as Ishmael was left to die. Abraham and Sarah's casting off of part of their family is seen on a massive scale in the way society has cast off part of the human family by ghettoizing persons of color and sending them out to fend for themselves in the economic wilderness of inequality.

Though some may say that things have surely changed since the days of slavery, and even since the years that Delores Williams penned her womanist reflections on Hagar in the early 1990s, the second decade of the twenty-first century saw rising levels of hate crimes against people of color and other minority groups, including against Muslims and Jews.[4] Unfortunately, today we still see part of our blended family cast out, while persons from certain groups continue to be harassed and feel their very lives are threatened, because of the racism, anti-Semitism, Islamophobia, and xenophobia that continue on today. We are all part of one blended human family, and there are many members of this larger human family who feel they are living in the wilderness because of the color of their skin or their religion or their country of origin.

If this seems too intense to talk about, it is important that we examine our own emotional reactions. It can be difficult for us to consider how some of us are treated better than others by society, because all of us have our own struggles and want to feel like we have "earned" our place in the world. We do not want to consider how we may have been the objects of society's favoritism by being part of the chosen race or born in the "right" country or to parents of the "right" religion. We want to see ourselves outside of any conditions that may have predisposed us for success, and instead focus on the limitations and challenges we have had to overcome.

Abraham and Sarah certainly had challenges to overcome. And yet, they were also wealthy enough to own slaves. In addition to having humans as property, they abused Hagar and cast her and Ishmael out into the wilderness. As people of faith, we are part of the larger family of faith that sees Abraham and Sarah as our forefather and foremother. As inheritors of the Christian religion, we are also privileged to be part of the world's largest religion. And though Christianity has countless divisions and sub-groups, the history of Christianity overall has shown Christians persecuting persons from other faith traditions. In this blended family, we are all implicated in casting out our brothers and sisters and dividing the family.

Embracing a Larger Blended Family

What would it look like to embrace one another as part of our extended family? One example comes to mind: a colleague of mine at Austin Seminary who teaches in New Testament. Dr. Margaret Aymer is originally from the Caribbean, and she is married to a white Frenchman, Laurent. She and Laurent are the parents of a six-year-old son, Gabriel. I interviewed Dr. Aymer because their family extends beyond the three of them: It also includes Gabriel's birth parents.

Dr. Aymer and her husband are adoptive parents. Because the adoption was open, they have known their child's birth parents since before he was born, and they have continued to keep in touch. Every year, both birth parents visit them, or her family goes to visit the birth parents in their respective homes. Her son's grandparents on his birth parents' side are also included in this larger family. Dr. Aymer asks them for traditions they want to pass along to Gabriel, and one set sent them homemade kolaches, a pastry handed down from Hungarian ancestors. By intentionally including their child's birth parents and extended family into their own family, Dr. Aymer and her husband are modeling an inclusive blended family.

Dr. Aymer explained to me, "My family is my immediate nuclear family: my husband, my son. And of course, my husband's parents are my in-laws. But my son's family is also kind of like in-laws. Because they are his family. So although they are not related to me, they are related to my son, so they are *his* family, so *they are people that matter*. That's the way I think about family in general, and I realize that a lot of Americans haven't had that modeled."

She pointed out the differences she sees between this arrangement and other understandings of family in society: "There's almost a sense of family as property in this kind of capitalist society where DNA is a means of marking which store each thing comes from and who it belongs to, rather than a sense that everybody's children is everybody's children and everybody has an opportunity and a responsibility to make sure kids get raised. My father's reaction to meeting my son's birth parents was to rhetorically adopt them, say, 'You're coming home with me. You're my kids now.' Which is so quintessentially Caribbean, I think, at least in my experience of the Caribbean, that I don't even think about it, it's the water I swim in."

And while Dr. Aymer is fine including others into her family, she is fully aware of the difficulties others have in seeing her as the mother of her child. As a Black woman adopting a white child, she knew what she was getting into. She said: "I knew from the very beginning, well before we finalized the adoption, that people would think I am the nanny. So I went into this with my eyes open. And, it doesn't usually take long, for people to figure that out [our relationship as mother and son]. I haven't had any negative comments thrown at me, directly, because of our relationship, because of me being Gabriel's mom. But I have had to explain to women of color that I didn't go looking for a white child. I wasn't objecting to having a white child, but I didn't go looking for one."

Dr. Aymer and her family participate in an open adoption, where their child was intentionally placed *with them, by the birth parents* of their child. Dr. Aymer shares: "It is always quite a moment when people get that he was placed with us. That we didn't choose the birth parents—the birth parents chose us. That's a very different reality than a child that was taken by the state and we went in and said 'we'll become the parents of this child.' That was not the case. We were chosen by the birth parents. And part of the reason why our relationship with the birth parents is so strong is that they established a relationship with us before they gave birth. . . . I have a deep love for my son's birth parents and would do anything I could to help them. Because I like them as people, and I told them even before he was born, 'If you choose to parent this child, this child will be raised by loving people and will be perfectly fine.' I was not under any illusions that he would have been under any danger if they had raised him. They were not prepared to parent, and they wanted to place [the child]. That was their choice."

Even while these circumstances seem ideal, Dr. Aymer calls adoption a "trauma." "Adoption is always at base a trauma. Whenever a baby is removed from the family of origin there is always a trauma, even if the baby can't express it." She does not know how Gabriel will react to his adoption as he gets older, but they will talk about it when it happens. In the meantime, Gabriel has known from the beginning, learning from picture books put together of all the different family members.

I asked her to share with me some of her experiences of witnessing her son navigating these different relationships. "It depends on the day. Most of the time I'm just Mommy, and Laurent is Papa. When we were with his birth mom the last time, I became 'fake mom.' She became 'real mom' because he was in her belly, that's what he said, and I let him go with it. I think shaming kids for making sense of their own world in language that makes sense for them—doesn't make any sense. He wasn't trying to be disrespectful, he was describing a relationship. He was saying 'I didn't come from your belly, I came from her belly. So she's my real mom and you're my fake mom.' When we landed in Texas, I became Mommy again. So, it is what it is.

"Because I'm a person of color, I come with a natural suspicion of the myths of America, like Thanksgiving and how that is portrayed. So when my child and I go to the public library, and he sees a book about the residential schools that Canadians sent their Indian children to, I didn't stop him from picking it up, even though I told him it was a very sad story. He wanted me to read it to him, which I did, and we talked about it, and he wanted to bring it home and read it again. He wanted to understand why it is that these people were mad at these kids for speaking their language, because of course, he's bilingual. So he doesn't understand the problem about speaking other languages, because everybody does it, right? So that was a good conversation to have.

"He has come to a very early realization that he has said out loud that because of his phenotype, racism, sexism, and xenophobia do not directly affect him. What we need to help him to understand is that it does affect him directly because it affects his parents. That because both of his parents are immigrants, xenophobia affects us both, and because his mother is a Black woman.

"But [after] that first realization, we talk about everything. I'm under the opinion that the more you tell them, the fewer mistakes they are likely to make, and he recently asked me about the 'n' word. Because he's beginning to learn bad words on the public school playground. I said to him, 'now you need to understand, that word is even worse than "mudblood" in Harry Potter.' And his eyes got as big as saucers. So we talk, and we try to figure it out.

"But that's it. Most of time it's just a regular family relationship. I mean, I'm Mom, there's Dad, he gets up in the morning, has his breakfast, goes off to school, comes back home, plays his piano and wants to play on his tablet, and you know, he's a kid!"

Living as Part of Humanity's Blended Family

We are all part of one human race, but our individual experiences within that human race are vastly different. We share many similarities: we breathe air, our hearts beat, we all love and experience loss, we all are born and eventually will die. But we also are very different from one another. The blended family of the human race is made up of people who have been divided along racial lines, even though the concept of race is not biological. Our experiences as humans have been shaped by the long history of racism in the United States and around the world. We have also been shaped by where we grew up and when. We are also different in how we present as male or female. Differences seemingly as mundane as height can influence how we are perceived and treated by others in society. The different ways people are treated because of the characteristics that describe us is bias, and there have been studies that show our biases being part of our snap judgments of others before we are conscious of them.[5]

The favoritism that we worried about above in the conversation about divine favoritism is present in our biases toward one another. We prefer persons who look like us and make us feel like we belong. We have strong in-group biases where we are drawn toward people who we see as being like us. Such bias, when played out over time, leads to some groups with more advantages, continuing to share those advantages among people who look like them. Combating our biases begins with becoming aware of them and consciously trying to change the ways we make decisions and share our resources. Who are we choosing to sit with? Where are we choosing to live or send our kids to school? Who are we deciding to hire for this position? Take a look at the decisions you make over time and see where your biases may be operating. Consider how you may be able to make different decisions by being open to the gifts of others who look different from you.

Questions for Reflection

1. Looking at the story of Abraham, Sarah, and Hagar, have you ever identified with Hagar in the story or considered her experiences? What do you think of Delores Williams's reading of Hagar as a story that resonates with women of color?

2. How is society a blended family? What are the ways you see some groups being treated better than others? Where do you see some members of the larger human family being "cast out"?

3. Do you have a "blended" family? What have been some of the challenges your family has gone through? Have there been times when people outside your family have had difficulty seeing you as a family?

4. How is the church a kind of blended family? How do you see your congregation bringing people into the "family"? Are there ways your church could do better at making everyone feel more equally part of this larger family?

5. Think about all the people in society in charge of taking care of children: nursery caregivers and teachers as well as parents. How well does society take care of those who care for children? What are some ways you can support the work of those who care for children and help them feel more included and valued by society?

Chapter 7

Who Will Save Isaac?

SCRIPTURE: GENESIS 22:1–19

Introduction

The story in Genesis 22:1–19 about the near sacrifice of Isaac, Abraham's son, which is also referred to as the Akedah ("the binding") in Judaism, constitutes one the most disturbing narratives in the Hebrew Bible. It is also considered one of the most central. Elie Wiesel writes, "To me the *Akeda* was an unfathomable mystery given to every generation, to be relived, if not solved. . . ."[1] Indeed, all of the three Abrahamic monotheisms—Judaism, Christianity, and Islam—have variations of this story whereby a beloved, chosen son is sacrificed or nearly sacrificed by the express command of God. The version of the sacrifice-of-the-beloved-son story that readers would be the most familiar with is probably the story of Jesus' sacrifice. Why is this story or variations of it so popular in Abrahamic traditions? Why do they hold up a variation of a disturbing story about the murder or near murder of a beloved child by his father as a core narrative of their faith? Moreover, how can we, as faithful readers, respect the centrality of these stories of child sacrifice in these traditions while also interrogating the problematic vision of the family that emerges from this tale?

The Significance of Isaac

In order to understand the significance of Isaac's near sacrifice we have to understand the significance of Isaac, the boy who is nearly killed. Isaac is the long-awaited son of the Israelite matriarch, Sarah. Sarah has had issues with infertility for so long that when we meet her in the text, she is already too old to have children. Like so many female characters in the biblical text, from the very moment we encounter Sarah, her concern is inevitably focused on this problem. As we discussed in a previous chapter, a woman without a male heir in the ancient Near East was in an extremely precarious position.

Not just Sarah, but the story itself in the biblical text, as framed through the experiences of these Israelite matriarchs and patriarchs, also has been eagerly awaiting and building to the birth of Isaac. From the very beginning of the narrative about Sarah and Abraham in Genesis 12, the focus of the narrative has been on whether this couple will have a child who will carry on the promise and covenant made between Abraham and God known as the Abrahamic promise. It is this long-awaited promised child—Isaac—who is finally born in Genesis 21 to the joy and surprise of his parents, especially his mother.

The Sacrifice of Isaac

As we observed in the previous section, the importance of Isaac cannot be overstated: He is both the hope of an entire nation and the precious, indeed miraculously conceived son of parents who had thought that having a child would be impossible. In this context the mere idea that he should be sacrificed is utterly shocking. Yet oddly after so joyously announcing the birth of this long-awaited child in Genesis 21, after elucidating the significance of Isaac, God, in the very next chapter, seeks to kill him. God inexplicably commands Abraham, Isaac's father, to take Isaac and sacrifice him as a whole burnt offering in Genesis 22:1-2. It seems that the narrative informs the reader of the miraculous birth of Isaac only to heighten the surprise and horror when, immediately thereafter, Isaac is commanded by God to be slaughtered. The type of offering that Isaac is supposed to constitute adds to the terror. This type of offering, a whole burnt offering, is also sometimes referred to as the holocaust offering, and it is one in which the entire animal is burnt up and sent as smoke as an offering to God. Indeed, the type of sacrifice commanded here is part of the reason why this narrative is sometimes seen as a prism through which to understand the Holocaust.

The narrative moreover heightens the sense of dread and anxiety by using particular words that stress the dearness of Isaac to Abraham, calling him "your son, your only son Isaac, whom you love" (v. 2). Considering that Abraham actually has another son, Ishmael, who was tragically sent away after Isaac's birth, the reference to Isaac as Abraham's "only son" undoubtedly points to the value of Isaac, and therefore to the magnitude of the demanded sacrifice. Isaac, because of the cycle of family dysfunction we've discussed in previous chapters of Genesis, is now the only child in the family. Moreover, considering the difficulties Sarah faced in getting pregnant, it is clear that Isaac will remain the only child that Sarah will ever have, and therefore will constitute, in the Hebrew Scriptures, the only heir to this promise made by God to Abraham.

This stress on the importance of Isaac is all the more telling and poignant when we realize that Genesis 22 is noted for its sparseness and reticence, telling the reader little to no information that would help readers make sense of the story. Things that readers would dearly like to know, such as the emotional and mental state of Abraham, and whether Isaac is a willing participant or an unwilling victim in this drama, are left ominously absent in the tale. Indeed, the text hints that Isaac might have had some idea of the dangerous situation he was in as it depicts Isaac asking his father about the whereabouts of the lamb that is to be sacrificed (v. 7). Forebodingly or faithfully, depending on one's interpretation, Abraham responds that God, himself, will provide the lamb for the offering (v. 8), both referencing God's initial call to sacrifice Isaac (v. 2) and also the conclusion of the story whereby an angel, at the very last moment, will offer a ram as Isaac's replacement (vv. 11–14).

The sparseness of the story, moreover, which is most clearly evident in the Hebrew, not only makes the motivations, thoughts, and portrayals of the characters murky, but it also adds to the terror of this text by cutting all the music and noise from the scene. The reader, therefore, is left to think and ponder in silence—a silence that is only punctuated by the thin and sparse words of the father and son, as one leads the other to his likely death.

Questions and Problems

In offering such a sparse narrative, the story offers no answers to the numerous theological and ethical riddles and dilemmas it presents. In so doing, the story compels the readers to wrestle with these issues themselves. And as evident, one of the key questions, which runs like a scarlet thread through the narrative, is: Why has God asked Abraham to do this unspeakable, unethical act? What is God trying to find out, and what information can be worth the price of someone's life?

The usual answer given, and which is supported at points by the biblical text, is that God was testing Abraham's faith or whether he fears

God. Indeed, at the end of this story, God states that God now knows that Abraham fears God because he has not withheld even his son (v. 12). Yet this narrative presents a disturbing, unsettling picture of God. Why does an all-powerful deity need to test Abraham's loyalty and devotion and respect so badly and in this manner? Even if such a test were necessary, couldn't God design a test that did not involve the death of a child? Is there so much insecurity about Abraham's loyalty and devotion that God has to devise a murder scheme where Abraham is forced to choose between his son or his God? What kind of God does this, and do we want to worship such a deity?

Other theological dilemmas are also present. If this test is about faith, it is unclear how the sacrifice addresses or defines faithfulness or fear of God exactly. Why and how does Abraham's willingness to kill his son without challenge indicate Abraham's faith in or respect for God? The only thing this "test" seems to show is that Abraham will blindly do whatever God commands no matter how destructive or unethical.

As such, this narrative naturally leads to multiple questions about theology and ethics. What constitutes faith or rightful fear of God? Does it consist of blind obedience, and what happens when the divine command contradicts human ethics? Which one takes precedence? And lest the reader be tempted to leap easily to the answer of God or God's commands as primary, remember that our natural ethical sense, as some have argued, might also stem from God. Why would God give people an understanding of right and wrong only to command them to commit heinous deeds—such as murdering one's child—that they know innately are wrong? Is abuse, be it of a family member, friend, animal, or anything, ever OK even if the abuse is commanded by God? And if so, how do we know if this commanded abuse stems from God or from some other source?

You may at this point be tempted to dismiss this story by stating that this is only in the Hebrew Bible / Old Testament and not in the New Testament, the testament that Christians silently and unwittingly favor. It is rather horrifying, I admit. And some in the church do have a tendency to dismiss disturbing tales in the Hebrew Scriptures and in so doing to treat them as if they are not part of the canon when it suits us. However, this particular narrative though part of the Hebrew canon is more difficult to ignore. As I noted earlier, Christianity too has a variation of this story. In the Christian tradition, God once again allows and indeed commands the murder of an innocent son, albeit a willing son in this case. Hence, even in the New Testament similar questions are raised about why and what kind of God would demand the murder of an innocent as a test of faith or fear. Even if the murder is for a "good" cause (although what this cause is in the case of Isaac is unclear!), it is problematic that an all-powerful God cannot devise a different solution, which would bring about the good effect caused by the sacrifice without recourse to murder.

Family Dynamics and This Story's Influence

In short, though we may want to, we cannot easily wiggle out of confronting the theological problems this story or its variants presents. And these problems and questions about God easily bleed into ones about the family. Not only is Abraham's silent and willing obedience to murder his child problematic, but if we imagine God as a parent, as many of us do, then this story is about the abuse and possible murder of a child by multiple parental or authority figures. And considering that this story is canonical and authoritative, and considering that Abraham is renowned for his faithfulness, in part, for attempting to follow through on the murder of his son, this story can be misread as allowing or permitting other abuses of those who are less powerful, like children.

One scholar, Carol Delaney, has argued as such. She writes that these stories about the divinely sanctioned murder and abuse of children and women, because they appear in a canonical text, sanction similar mistreatment of the powerless in the world.[2] The biblical text, Delaney argues, as a fundamental text, therefore normalizes and allows abuse. Indeed, Delaney cites a case when a similar event happened. In 1990, a California man claimed to have heard God's voice commanding him to sacrifice his youngest daughter and followed through. What separates this man from Abraham, Delaney asks? And if there is little to separate them, how can we laud Abraham (and God) and yet condemn this man or other people who commit similar acts as either insane or criminal? Indeed, the main difference between Abraham and this man in California seems to be that Abraham is provided an animal substitute in Genesis 22, an unusual occurrence in the biblical text wherein other child sacrifices are enacted with little resistance or pause (cf. Judg. 11:34–40; 2 Kgs. 3:27). Indeed, even in Genesis 22 there might be a hint that Abraham followed through with God's command. It states ominously in Genesis 22:19 that Abraham returned to his servants, and they went back to Beersheba with no mention of the whereabouts or the presence of Isaac.

Delaney's argument should make us reconsider Abraham as a model of faith. Although Abraham is the patriarch of the three Abrahamic monotheisms (Judaism, Christianity, and Islam), perhaps we should reimagine him as a model, at times, of what *not* to do—as an anti-model instead. Rather than praising Abraham for passively ceding to God's command, perhaps we should instead interrogate his actions and declare that he instead should have argued back, questioned God, and resisted God's unethical command. Indeed, some interpreters have even argued that Abraham in Genesis 22 does *not* actually pass the test. He may pass the test if faith and fear are defined as blind obedience, but he does *not* pass the larger, unstated test about how one should behave when confronted with such an ethical dilemma. Instead of blindly obeying, he should have argued against God as he did earlier when God decided to destroy the cities of Sodom and Gomorrah (Gen. 18:17–33), or he should have pleaded with God for the life of his son.

In terms of the family, Abraham's lack of communication with his partner, Sarah, is also disturbing and is also characteristic of an anti-model. Sarah's whereabouts and her knowledge of the ordeal are entirely missing from the biblical text. Where is Sarah, and did she know what Abraham was up to? It seems unlikely that Sarah would have remained so uninvolved had she been informed that Abraham was going to take her child and kill him. Abraham seems to have decided that Sarah did not need to be informed about this command from God and therefore, did not include her in discussions about the welfare of their child. Unfortunately, as we saw in previous chapters, this is not the first time that Abraham is irritatingly reticent and uncommunicative with his spouse. Considering that, immediately after this story, Sarah promptly dies (Gen. 23:1–2), interpreters have wondered whether her death was the result of Sarah's discovery of her husband's secret attempt to murder their child—the child that she has spent her whole life waiting for. If so, then this demonstrates the ways in which dysfunction and abuse reverberates throughout the family unit, multiplying the victims. There are not just one but two victims of Abraham's deed—Isaac and Sarah.

Sarah's lack of knowledge speaks to modern instances where one parent remains in the dark about the secret, hidden abuses committed by other members in the family. Though I am not arguing that Abraham was secretly abusing Isaac in Genesis 22, his lack of communication with Sarah and his silent ceding to God's command to kill his child does indicate that we should read and see in his family, not as a model, but as an anti-model of a healthy family unit. Indeed, there is evidence that this family dysfunction caused great trauma and a fracturing of family relationships. Aside from Sarah's demise, Isaac never again speaks directly to his father after Genesis 22 and seems deeply dismayed over the death of his mother (Gen. 24:67). Perhaps Genesis 22:19 speaks of only Abraham returning without Isaac to indicate, not Isaac's death, but his separation from his father after this event. Perhaps it symbolizes Isaac's psychological transformation. The text does not mention Isaac because the old Isaac never returned to Beersheba with his father.[3] Moreover, unlike other Israelite patriarchs such as Jacob, for some reason, Isaac, does not seek and find his own wife. Rather, a wife has be sought out and brought to him by his father's servant, hinting that he may be unfit or incapable of going out (Gen. 24). All this suggests the lingering effects of trauma.

It also might hint of survival and hope. The famous author Elie Wiesel writes that it is telling that Isaac's name means laughter in Hebrew. This is especially odd considering that the most famous story connected to Isaac is that of his near murder. Wiesel writes that Isaac is named "laughter" because he survived and carried on after his ordeal. Despite being nearly killed by God and a family member, by those whom he trusted, Isaac still lived on and learned to laugh again. In so doing, Isaac, as Wiesel interprets this figure, offers us a model of hope. We too, no matter our traumas, problems, or abuse, can survive and live and laugh as Isaac did: "Why was the most tragic of our ancestors named Isaac, a name which evokes and signifies laughter? Here is why. As the first survivor, he had to teach us, the future survivors of Jewish history, that it is possible to suffer and despair an entire lifetime and still not give up the art of laughter."[4]

Reconsiderations of the Story

Like other important narratives in the Hebrew Bible—the most famous of which is Job—the point of the story about the sacrifice of Isaac is not to offer answers but to push us to ask questions. And in asking them, the narrative forces readers to reconsider, to not take anything as a given, and, in so doing, to come to a deeper, more ambivalent, albeit unsettled understanding of God and the nature of the world, including the family. For example, if this story is indeed about faith, then its purpose might be to show that faith is something more than unconsidered obedience and imitation. We are *not* simply to mime Abraham and obey God no matter the ethical problems of a divine request. Rather, the point of the narrative might be to demand that the readers readjust, redefine, and enlarge our understanding of faith and of fear. Perhaps faith in or respect for God is not blindly following but speaking and indeed arguing back when the demands are abhorrent or unconscionable. Perhaps faith entails standing up to God. Indeed, if we enlarge Isaac as symbolic of any child or powerless individual, this story can be read as about the need to protect anyone and everyone who is endangered or oppressed or "sacrificed," especially by those who justify their abuses in the name of God. This is the true way to pass the test, the story suggests.

This test moreover might not just be ours alone. Such instances of continued "sacrifices" of the various Isaacs in our world can also be read as a test of God and therefore by extension as a test of the communities of faith that claim God as their head. Will God and God's people let God's children be murdered, abused, oppressed, and sacrificed? If so, for how long? In this instance in Genesis 22, we are given hope that sometimes, at least in our authoritative Scriptures, God steps in and says no and stops the sacrifice—that at times God, and therefore God's people, can also pass the test.

Talking about Isaac Today

The story of Abraham being tested by God may not seem relevant to life struggles of families today. Human sacrifices? Who does *that*?

But imagine a different scenario: you are part of a religious tradition that says being gay is a choice and a sin, and that to accept someone as gay means you are going to hell. Imagine being part of a church community like that, and then hearing from your child that they are gay. What do you do? Do you accept your child as they are and support them? Or do you react with the messages you have heard from your church, that being gay is a phase or a choice and that they need to resist this, or even go to therapy?

While God telling Abraham to kill his own son seems like an extreme example for a test of faith, parents today continue to feel "tested" by their religion when their children come out to them as gay, lesbian, bisexual, or transgender. When families are deeply involved with a congregation that preaches the view that God is against being LGBTQ, the message that their child is gay can appear like a test of faith. Who do they listen to? The voice of "God" as expressed by their pastor and their church? Or the voice of their child who needs their love and support?

One of my former students, Susan Cottrell, went through this test of faith. Susan regularly shares her story with others, knowing she is not alone in having spent time committed to a church family that believes being LGBTQ is against God's will. She and her husband, Rob, raised their five children in an evangelical church community for over twenty years. The church was a huge part of their lives.

Susan told me about the day that everything changed. "Annie called me from college. She was twenty years old. I was cleaning the bathroom when Annie said, 'Mom, I've got something to tell you. I'm attracted to girls. I think I'm bisexual. I've prayed about it, Mom, I've resisted it. But it won't go away.' My immediate thoughts were, 'What will become of her? Will she ever love and be loved like her dad and I love each other? And *we'll never be the same in the church.*' I found that final thought deeply disturbing. After all, church is meant to be a safe place, family. And I knew it wouldn't be."[5] Instead of celebrating her daughter, Susan was afraid for her and felt she had to protect her. She had nothing against the LGBTQ community, she said, but having spent twenty years in the evangelical church, she had internalized that being gay was somehow wrong. Susan encouraged Annie to continue to resist being bisexual— something they both thought God wanted. But that was untenable, and within months, Annie said she was dating women and was "more at peace with God than she'd ever been." Susan said, "That's the whole point. I knew she was on the right track, and it gave me peace too." She was also shocked to learn how specious the biblical case against being LGBTQ was. She knew that countless families were suffering church rejection and poor teaching, and she felt the call to help them.

Susan started a nonprofit organization called FreedHearts, to support parents and families of LGBTQ children and adults. Susan's organization supports the gay community by reconciling faith issues and serving as a surrogate parent for many people who have been rejected by their own families and churches. Susan's talks in person and online have enabled her to connect with people all over the world who want to know how to support their LGBTQ children and with LGBTQ people who are glad to have an example to set for their parents of a mother who affirms them and loves them, and want help with religious, family, and community wounds.

For parents today who feel God is testing them by asking them to give up their son or daughter who is LGBTQ, it is important for them to know there are other examples of people of faith who are choosing a different way. There are countless examples of Christians who are able to represent God's work of love in the world. Parents who have changed their minds because of having an LGBTQ child are eager to try and share that love with others: Parents do not have to sacrifice their children in order to be faithful people. They can live out their faith by trusting that the God who enabled the miracle of life to take hold in their children is continuing to desire their flourishing as full human beings, not stunted or repressed or hidden.

This conversation may still be hard for many who may not have a child who is LGBTQ, and who are part of denominations that hold anti-LGBTQ positions. If you are a member or a church leader in a denomination that does not support LGBTQ persons by preventing them from being ordained or serving in leadership or getting married in your church, what are you being called on to do? If your denomination is holding a major vote over whether or not to accept LGBTQ persons and ordain them as pastors and conduct same-sex weddings, do you speak out and sacrifice your own position as a church leader? Or do you remain silent in order to keep your influence and power intact? Even if you do not have a child who is LGBTQ, perhaps you know someone who is, and who is called to ministry. What will you sacrifice in order to support them?

If you are part of a more liberal Christian denomination such as the United Church of Christ, the Episcopal Church, or the Presbyterian Church (U.S.A.), this may not be your experience. Some of these denominations have been ordaining LGBTQ persons for many years. But even within more liberal mainline denominations, there are many conservative churches where the congregation may still be hesitant to support LGBTQ persons, host gay weddings in their sanctuary, or hire a gay pastor, even if the official stance of the denomination is more progressive. The United Methodist Church (UMC), considered a "mainline" denomination and the second-largest denomination in the United States behind Southern Baptists, voted in 2019 to retain more traditional language in its book of rules for who can be ordained or married in its churches, which meant banning LGBTQ persons from being ordained or married by their pastors. As of November 2019, there were rumors that the UMC may split over the issue.[6]

Churches that split can feel very much like a family going through a divorce. It is painful. People pick sides. Emotions rise and people say things that hurt one another. But staying together may just be too painful for everyone involved.

Relating to the Biblical Text

I wonder if that is what Sarah felt, that it was just too painful to stay together, after Abraham returned and told her what had happened. The biblical narrative doesn't tell us what happened when he came back, or why Isaac didn't come back with him, or why we don't hear about Sarah again until her death. But the choice to sacrifice his son cost Abraham everything. The biblical writers make him out to be a hero of the faith, of having passed a test, conveying an image of God that commanded the sacrifice and approved of Abraham's actions. What if this story was influenced by other religions of the era that commanded human child sacrifices to appease the gods? What if the early narrators of this story thought they were trying to show that the God of Abraham was kind of like all of the other gods and yet also different? Because God, in the end, did not require the sacrifice. God instead stopped it from happening.

I would like to think that God never intended Abraham to go through with it in the first place, that this was a mistake on Abraham's part to even consider it. I would like to think that there have been so many mistakes Christians have made over the years, about slavery, about war, about women, and that this story is an example of the kind of major mistakes in interpretation that religious people can make: that they can perceive God asking them to do things that do real damage to other human beings, but if they are listening closely enough, they will hear God trying to stop them.

Rachel Held Evans was a young woman living in Dayton, Tennessee, having grown up the child of a Bible college professor and spending her teen years immersed in evangelical church culture. She died in 2019 unexpectedly after a brief illness. Her passing was mourned by the many who saw in her a new way to live as a Christian. One of her bestselling books, *Searching for Sunday*, chronicles her path from the evangelical faith of her upbringing to the Episcopal church she started attending after a long struggle of losing faith in the church that had formed her in her faith.[7]

As she began to question some of the tenets of her faith as a college student, she felt her church wanting to shut down her questions. She began to blog about the questions she had about what she had grown up learning, including views about the role of women in the church and the nonacceptance of LGBTQ persons. Eventually, after a long heartfelt conversation with her pastor, she decided to leave her church. It was a painful experience of letting go. After some time, she found her place within a new worshiping community affiliated with the Episcopal Church. Along the way, she discovered online that there were many other people who had the same questions she did, and many who also had to leave their church communities in order to find acceptance.

Through her writing and speaking, Rachel Held Evans became a beacon for many who were looking for ways of being a Christian that did not mean they had to reject part of themselves or part of their family. One reader of her blog reached out to share his story of coming out to his dad who was a pastor. Andrew grew up in a fundamentalist Presbyterian church where his dad preached that gay people were going to hell. When he started having feelings of attraction toward other boys, he began praying about it and journaled about his fears: "I'm so scared. I don't want to be an outcast. . . . Do you care what I'm going through, God? Why did you make me this way? What are you trying to teach me, God? I lift my hands to you. I'm in your hands. . . . Give me faith! Please! I can't hold on much longer."[8]

He eventually accepted his orientation and found a Christian community who celebrated him for who he was. Like Rachel, he found a different community of faith who was open to accepting him just as he was. Andrew told Rachel that he was excited about being baptized, looking forward to this event that had been denied to him for so long because he was told he wasn't good enough. Now that he had found a church that affirmed for him that God's grace was enough, and that he was enough, Andrew wanted to share that with others. He asked Rachel to attend his baptism, and she saw the invitation as significant. It was so important to him because "I was part of the only family he had."[9]

When a child is baptized, the community of faith usually sees up front not only the one being baptized, but the parents and family as well. Baptism is a sign of commitment on the part of all there to witness it: the congregation is asked to promise to raise this child in the faith and to support and love this child. A person who identifies as LGBTQ is God's child in every way. The person's immediate family and family of faith play important roles in shaping that person in the faith and helping them grow up knowing God's love. If we do not play that role well, we risk paying a heavy price: ostracizing a member of our family or a member of our church family, perhaps losing out on being in relationship with them. Ultimately, we would miss out on the gifts we could receive from remaining in relationship with this child of God.

There are Christian churches and communities that have formed specifically in response to the exclusion LGBTQ persons have faced from other denominations, and there are many churches in mainline denominations that make clear that they gladly welcome all people, specifically mentioning LGBTQ people. But for persons who remain in churches and denominations that hesitate to offer this kind of welcome, what is the sacrifice?

Rethinking the Abraham and Isaac story means rethinking our assumptions about what sacrifices we are being asked to make for our faith. Rather than believing God is calling us to sacrifice a significant relationship, either of a child or a member of our church family because of who they are, we need to question our beliefs and question our reading of the Bible. Remembering that the Bible is not God, and that our relationship with the Bible is not the same as our relationship with God, we can pray for God's wisdom to better understand how to relate to one another in love.

At the same time, if we are part of traditions that fully celebrate the inclusion of LGBTQ people, we also need to reconsider our relationships with family members who are not yet there. It is easy for Christians to judge one another; both conservatives and liberals can be judgmental. For persons who have not always been supportive of LGBTQ people, it is important to remember our own journey of change, and to remember we have not always had the beliefs we have now. This is not to say we should be silent when others are expressing anti-LGBTQ views, but it is to say we should not come at others with a sense of self-righteousness. Sharing stories about your own process of challenging assumptions can help others learn how you changed. It may not change others' minds, but it may help them better understand your journey. People change slowly, over time, and one story may help lead to another story, and as time unfolds those stories may build to a crescendo of voices.

We cannot hear Isaac's voice from this passage. We do not know what he said after this event or if he ever spoke to his father again. But we do have the opportunity to listen to the voices of people today whose families have sacrificed their children for the sake of their religion. The stories these voices tell are painful. And yet, when parents choose *not* to sacrifice their children, and instead choose to love their children as they are, the stories of human flourishing abound.

Questions for Reflection

1. What have been your reactions to reading Genesis 22 in the past? How did reading it make you feel?
2. How does it feel to challenge the story and to critique Abraham, and even God, in the story?

3. The second half of this chapter focuses on parents who feel they are asked to sacrifice their relationship with their children who come out as LGBTQ. Do these stories relate to your experiences at all? What is your church's position on what it means to be LGBTQ?

4. Lifting up the silenced voices in Scripture allows us to listen to the voices of persons today who have been silenced. Do you feel there are persons who are silenced in your congregation? Who feel they have had to sacrifice part of their identity in order to be part of your community?

5. Are there other reasons why parents may feel they are being asked to "sacrifice" their children for the sake of the church or their belief in God? Are there persons you know who feel their parents chose their faith community or church or understanding of God over choosing to love them?

6. Is the language of sacrifice meaningful to you in your own family or church community? How can it be used in ways that are not harmful?

7. Do you know of parents or individuals who have chosen love over sacrificing their relationship with a loved one? In what ways did that come at a cost in their community? In what ways did you see them flourish?

Chapter 8

The Traps of Competitive Parenting

Keeping Up with Rachel and Leah

SCRIPTURE: GENESIS 29:1–30:24

Introduction

Though just as important as Abraham, Isaac, and Jacob, the matriarchs of Israel and their stories are less well-known, especially in the church. Despite this lack of recognition, the matriarchs play a key role in constituting and building up the family of Israel. Through the stories of their relationships and interactions in the family, these matriarchs moreover have a fundamental role in how families are portrayed and envisioned in the biblical text. As a result, they are crucial to the paradigm of the family that emerges from the Hebrew biblical text. In another story about the family of Israel in Genesis, we are confronted with two matriarchs, Rachel and Leah, sisters who are both married to Jacob, the third and last patriarch. Though this story is set in a context in which polygamy was accepted, the sibling relationship of Jacob's two wives should alert the reader that much drama and competitiveness will inevitably follow. Hence, the story of Leah and Rachel not only is connected to and continues the rivalrous sibling relationships that we have seen in other parts of the biblical text, but their contest will serve as an appropriate lens by which to reflect on modern issues, such as parental competition, that concern the family.

The Introduction of Leah and Rachel

Leah and Rachel's story begins and intertwines with that of their husband, Jacob. We meet these characters when Jacob meets them, and the order and nature of their meetings set up and explain the competition between the sisters that will follow and that will climax with their "birthing contest" in Genesis 30.

Jacob, the patriarch of Israel, whose name will be later changed by God to "Israel," first meets Rachel, the second, younger daughter of his uncle, Laban, after leaving his family in Canaan. In the preceding chapters of Genesis, we learn that Jacob has to leave his family because of his own rivalry with his twin brother, Esau, who is born a few moments earlier than Jacob. This competition culminates in Jacob's exchange of Esau's birthright—the double portion of inheritance that goes to the firstborn—for some stew (Gen. 25:29–34), and Jacob's theft of Esau's blessing from his father, Isaac (27:1–40). Though we will discuss the stories of the rivalry between these brothers in the next chapter of the book, needless to say, Jacob's actions so incense and anger Esau that Jacob, under the advice of his parents, has to leave his family home to make his life elsewhere (27:41–45). It is therefore sibling competition that drives Jacob to journey to Aram in Syria, the area where his mother is from, where he will meet his cousins, Leah and Rachel, who will later become his rivalrous wives.

The reason for Jacob's journey—sibling rivalry and contest—as well as the parental favoritisms that undergird these competitions will set a pattern of dysfunctional family relationships that will shape the stories of the first families of Israel. The competition between the twin brothers will inevitably be reflected in and continued by the competition between the sisters, Rachel and Leah, who will become Jacob's wives. Through these references, the stories show the ways in which family dynamics, especially unhealthy ones, have a lingering effect, reverberating throughout the generations. Indeed, competition and rivalry will be a family trait that this particular group will spend the rest of Genesis trying to work through and come to terms with.

After leaving his home, Jacob again finds himself in Aram, near a well, a favorite gathering place for women and an apt symbol of life and fertility because of its connection to water. There, in a romantic scene, Jacob, the younger son, sees Rachel, the younger daughter of Laban, his uncle, and is immediately smitten. He kisses her, weeps, and decides to marry Rachel (29:10–11). Unlike in the West, cross-cousin marriages were seen as entirely appropriate in this context, perhaps even ideal, as these marriages would be "distant" enough not to constitute incest but "close" enough to allow resources to be kept within the family.

Having found the perfect woman—indeed, Rachel and Jacob are portrayed very similarly, both depicted as tricky, rule-breaking, second-born children—Jacob immediately makes an agreement with her father, his uncle, that he will work seven years to make Rachel his wife. Though Laban seems happy with the agreement, emphasizing how Jacob is already family (29:14), considering the competitive and rivalrous nature of this particular family, Laban's remark hints that things are about to go awry and that more rivalries will follow.

And indeed they do. We are told that Rachel has an older sister named Leah. While Rachel, whose name means "ewe," is described as beautiful in form, Leah, whose name means "wild cow," is oddly described in Hebrew as having weak or soft eyes (29:17). It is unclear whether this description of Leah is positive—that she had beautiful eyes, which were like the lovely eyes of a cow—or negative. Indeed, some interpreters wonder if this description indicates something physically wrong with Leah, that Leah "needed glasses," so to speak.

Regardless of the exact meaning of Leah's description, it is clear that Leah and Rachel are portrayed as contrasts or opposites. Rachel is the beautiful, younger daughter who is beloved by Jacob. In contrast, Leah must therefore be the opposite: the less comely, older sister who, when we fill in the narrative holes, therefore is and will remain unloved by the same man. As we will see in the next chapter, this contrasting characterization of the sisters mimics a similar oppositional characterization of their husband, Jacob, and his twin brother, Esau.

The Exchange and the Background of the Rivalry

The disregard of Leah by Jacob, which will serve to undergird her rivalry with her sister, will be heightened by the duplicitous actions of her father, Laban. After working seven years in order to marry Rachel, we are told that, on the night of Jacob's wedding, Laban exchanges Leah for Rachel. For some reason, Jacob does not recognize that the wrong woman is in the tent until morning after the marriage is consummated. This "exchange" is mysteriously explained by Laban to the surprised and likely angry Jacob the next day as simply the way things are done: that in this country, the younger is not put before the firstborn (29:26). Many interpreters see Laban's response as narrative comeuppance for Jacob's earlier dupe of his poor blind father, Isaac, to obtain Esau's blessing (27:1–40). This theft constituted an instance in which Isaac was deceived by Jacob to put the younger, himself, before the firstborn, his brother.

Because of this narrative corrective, Jacob works for Laban for another seven years in order to marry Rachel, whom, the text emphasizes, he loved more than Leah (29:30). Needless to say, their father's deceptive exchange during the wedding night, which causes Rachel and Leah to both become wives to the same man, exacerbates the rivalrous relationship of the sisters who are already compared and contrasted in the text. Married to the same person, these competitive sisters now have the misfortune of being rivalrous wives who have to compete for family status and for the love and regard of the same man.

The deceptive manner in which Laban compels Jacob to marry the older, less-regarded Leah undoubtedly puts her in an unfortunate, almost tragic situation, and leaves her in a loveless marriage with a husband who never wanted to marry her in the first place. Laban's action moreover will mar the entire family as it helps to sow the seeds of disunity and competitiveness that will remain unresolved until the end of Genesis. Laban's duplicitous action for which he gained another seven years of free labor from Jacob will hurt not just Leah but also his other daughter, Rachel, who also faces her own difficulties. Though prettier, beloved, and desired by her husband, she has trouble getting pregnant. God, seeing that Leah is unloved, mysteriously decides to open up Leah's womb, making her super fertile (29:31). Rachel, meanwhile, in contrast to her sister, remains infertile. By heightening Leah's reproductive ability, God exacerbates the competition between the sibling-wives as God did with Cain and Abel.

The Birthing Contest

As we noted earlier, the measure of a woman in the patriarchal ancient Near Eastern context of the Bible centered on her ability to have sons. The portrayal of Rachel, the beloved wife struggling with infertility, and Leah, the unloved, fertile wife, fits the literary tropes and patterns of the biblical text. Repeatedly, the biblical text portrays the beloved wives, such as Sarah (Gen. 16:1), Rebekah (Gen. 25:21), Hannah (1 Sam. 1:2), Samson's mother (Judg. 13:2), and now Rachel, as being initially infertile in order to stress the specialness of the child.

Yet despite the stimulating drama provided by the use of this trope, the constant and easy focus on the female body in a text written and edited by groups of elite male scribes is disturbing. This is especially the case if we imagine ourselves in the place of these women who are forced in the text to struggle and compete with each other to obtain the thing they lack, which is easily possessed by the other: For Leah, this is the love and regard of her husband; and for Rachel, male heirs who will allow her some security and also help to maintain her position in the family. One woman has love but no children; and the other, children but no love.

Indeed, not just the male writers, but the male characters are depicted as exacerbating and creating fissures between these women. The unequal regard of his wives by Jacob which is countered by the women's unequal ability to have children by God heightens Leah and Rachel's contest. As evident, the machinations of the male characters in this story—Laban, Jacob, and even God who is also envisioned as a male figure throughout almost the entirety of Hebrew biblical text—thus lead to a desperate and rather heart-wrenching birthing battle between the two female characters as both women try to have as many sons as possible.

The actions of these women evince the helplessness and distress they feel. Rachel, who remains childless, becomes so desperate that she gives her maidservant to her husband as her proxy. Leah, after her childbearing slows, does the same by giving Jacob her maidservant as well. We know from the earlier story about Sarah and Hagar (Gen. 16) that giving your slave women as a substitute to your husband was an emotional and politically fraught action as it had the potential to lead to a readjustment of status among the female members of the family. It was, in short, an act of desperation.

Rachel and Leah's voices and feelings, which are largely missing from the text, are conveyed by the names they give to their children in Genesis 30. These children's names allude to, unsurprisingly, the competition between the sisters (v. 8), the hope that the woman's husband will respect and honor them (v. 20), and the hope that God will vindicate or reward the person (vv. 6, 23). The names in short allude to the harrowing situation that the women have been forced into by their father, husband, God, and the patriarchal society of which they are members—a society in which two women, who are sisters, have to compete for the regard of an important male figure, their husband, by reproducing as many male children as possible.

Though this competition would lead to the many sons needed to constitute the tribes of Israel, this birthing contest would have tragic results. Rachel will die in distress and pain while giving birth to her second son, Benjamin, en route back to Canaan (Gen. 35:16–20). And Leah, after the death of her sister, is never heard from again in the biblical text. Literarily, Leah too seems to have "died" when her sister did. Indeed, the competition between the sisters is even more tragic when we realize that, outside of the birthing contest, they were depicted as a cohesive unit, as family, even speaking as one voice, especially against the machinations of their father (Gen. 31:14-16). Compelled to compete with each other by their father, husband, and God, Rachel and Leah elucidate the harmful effects of patriarchy on women, children, and the family unit.

The Negative Effects of Competition and Rivalries

The story of Rachel and Leah's complex relationship and rivalry, though ancient, elucidates and speaks to issues and problems that continue to plague us today. For example, the competition between Leah and Rachel leads us to consider modern-day competitions among parents. Such competitions might not be as centered on the number of sons or the status of the wife in polygamous marriages as in the biblical text, but they still occur when parents use their children and their achievements as a means by which to obtain or maintain status in society.

Equally significant, their story leads us to think about the frequently written topic of competition among women. As is evident from the story, sexism and patriarchy force women to compete with each other, something that both the biblical story as well as modern accounts indicate as leading to deep distress for women and also to the family unit as a whole.[1] Concerns about patriarchy as they affect women and the family are related to the questions about the rightful role of women and relatedly, of men in society, a complex issue, which as evident from discussions of "mommy wars" and stay-at-home dads that are still being debated today.

Even the discussion of the topic of competition between women is fraught as it could misleadingly portray women as catty or aggressive, or aid to judge and stigmatize women for the same activities that men frequently engage in. Indeed, by focusing on female competition as the writers of the text do in this story, we, the readers, too might be made complicit in their patriarchal attempt to portray women as uncooperative, aggressive, and treacherous, even against their own family. As evident, the canonicity of these stories places a heavy responsibility on the reader. It compels us to think about how to engage in rightful interpretations that respect the text. Yet in so doing, we must be alert and not be lulled into easy acceptance of deplorable situations, especially ones that concern the family, which are described by the text and, at times, even upheld by it.

Competitive Parenting Today

As we've seen from the story of Rachel and Leah, these two women were not fighting simply out of jealousy; they had been brought together by the forces of patriarchy and unfair expectations to compete for love. What comes across as a race to procreate, the two women try to outdo one another in producing heirs: the only way they felt they could "count" in the grand ledger of human worth.

Fast-forward to today. Parenting is very different than it was in the ancient world. People do not try to outdo one another in how many children they are able to have. And yet, are there some comparisons to the ways parents today feel pressure to have their children succeed? In the biblical world, simply having children could be a miracle, quite literally. In today's world, having children is still seen as miraculous, but it is not enough. For them to succeed in a global marketplace of fierce competition is another miracle altogether. Wealth and income inequality around the world make couples trying to raise a family compete for what seem like scarce resources: good schools, good neighborhoods, good opportunities for their children so they can grow up to be successful and be able to support themselves. On top of these pressures, there are cultural expectations about the "right way" to raise a child and to parents, and what it means to be a "good mom" or a "good dad." Parents today may not be competing to outdo one another in having as many children as they can, but they may still be competing for a sense of significance and self-worth.

Imagine Rachel and Leah today as moms in a neighborhood known for these coveted resources: excellent schools with high ratings and plenty of opportunities for after-school activities. And while they may have been able to have children, they are faced with the pressures of raising these children into healthy, brilliant, emotionally intelligent, and well-rounded young people who can gain access to one of the few spots available in elite colleges around the country. On top of that, they are being asked to volunteer in the schools, help raise money for school activities, and show they are savvy about current parenting practices by limiting screen time and monitoring their children's nutritional and media diets. No small feat.

And all of this costs money. Parents today are told to start saving early for their children's education fund, to begin planning for higher education costs even as their children are still in diapers. The costs of a college education, the supposed ticket to a solid-middle-class existence, currently costs more than a house. And yet even if the money is somehow raised in time, getting into a top college may be another long shot. In order to secure this achievement, parents must do double duty: not only seeking their child's well-being through providing food, shelter, and attention to their physical and psychological health, but also serving as their child's mentor and coach, directing him or her toward the best activities that might help him or her stand out on a college application. Competitive parenting is not just for women: Men are jockeying for their child's place on elite soccer teams or arranging for special internships, so their child has a better chance of standing out.

For Rachel and Leah, their worth consisted in whether they could have babies and raise up a nation. For parents today, some feel their worth consists of whether their children will succeed by getting into an elite college and getting a good job. Competitive parenting for Rachel and Leah meant that their worth was tied to the number of heirs they could bear. For parents today, competitive parenting is the sense that parents' worth relies on ensuring their child's success.

However, that is not the story for all parents. There are some who are simply struggling to get by themselves, and their hopes for their children consist in them staying out of trouble and out of jail. For these families, the competition is less with other wealthy parents and instead with the forces of poverty as they try to keep their own heads above water.

In his 2015 book *Our Kids*, Robert Putnam pointed to a two-tier system of families in the United States today based not only on class but also on opportunities.[2] Those in the higher bracket included families that had two income earners, and those in the lower were composed of kaleidoscopic families—kids who may live with a single parent who might have multiple partners and multiple children from different partners sometimes living together, none of whom may have a steady job or earn a livable wage. The difference in the two tiers was primarily one of class: Even in families of the same race, those of an upper-class background were much more likely to have access to opportunities that might lead them to succeed. The other difference, impacted by class, but also distinct from it, was that of opportunity. Putnam looked at differences in class from his small hometown in Ohio from the middle of the twentieth century and saw that persons coming from less wealth were able to achieve higher status than their parents. Today, however, the class divide is more extreme and limits the opportunities for those from lower-class backgrounds. Fewer opportunities to succeed make it less likely that young people coming from poverty today can break out of the poverty they grew up in.

One of the ways class was shown to impact opportunities for children included styles of parenting. For parents who are stretched thin by working low-wage jobs at odd hours, their parenting approach is very different from parents who may have the ability to work from home, work fewer hours, or may even have one parent stay at home. Such differences could be seen at a basic level: how many words were spoken to a child in their early years. Parents with a higher level of education and greater job stability spoke nineteen million more words to their children by the time they had entered kindergarten than working-class parents and thirty-four million more words than parents on welfare.[3] Parents who had greater financial resources were more able to have the emotional and mental bandwidth to interact with their children, responding to a child's signals and verbal cues, a skill crucial to early childhood brain development. Such parents were more likely to devote time to reading to their children and eating dinner together on a regular basis. Parents who had to work late shifts or had unpredictable work schedules were less able to have meals together with their children or the time to talk about what was going on in their child's life. With greater stress in one's work and less financial security, a parent has a diminished capacity to care for the emotional and psychological needs of their child.

Putnam's research also looked at the difference in schools available to parents across social class, and found the results staggering. Children coming from poverty, put in schools surrounded by other children from poverty, were much less likely to do well academically than children from poverty who were able to attend schools surrounded by wealthier children. Wealthier children had parents who invested in the schools, who could volunteer to support teachers and raise funds for extra supplies in the classroom, and who were able to monitor their own children's academic success. Poor children attending these schools were more likely to have access to support systems and counselors who could help them catch up when their academic success lagged behind their better-off peers. Schools in poverty stricken areas, however, had none of these resources. Parents were not able to be involved in the schools because they were too busy trying to earn a living wage, and they had no extra funds to help raise money for classroom activities. If such schools have full-time counselors, they are too often directed toward breaking up fights and responding to behavioral problems more than supporting students who need academic help.

The third major difference between the rich and poor in Putnam's study was in access to supportive communities. Children who grow up in wealthier neighborhoods tend to have parents who have close friends, which means that kids have a larger network of supportive adults in the area looking out for them. These children may also be part of religious communities, another source of emotional support for the families. These relationships also provide countless opportunities for informal mentoring, where children learn from the adults around them about the possibilities they might have open to them in the future. On the other hand, kids growing up in poorer neighborhoods have fewer adults they can turn to as role models or supportive figures. With higher rates of crime and violence in poorer neighborhoods, children growing up in poverty have a greater likelihood of being exposed to negative influences and being traumatized by the violence they encounter.

Putnam's book is full of in-depth interviews with people growing up in both of these contexts. The stories come from people of different races and ethnicities, and those who come from a more stable family background with a steady income tended to fare much better than those who came from households where parents were not able to be as involved in their children's lives because of personal difficulties such as unemployment or addiction. The opportunities available to children from wealthier families were exponentially higher than those available to children from poorer families.

From Putnam's research, it seems obvious that economics plays such an outsized role in the well-being of children and their opportunities for flourishing. It should come as no surprise, then, that some parents are willing to leave their children in order to better provide for them.

In his book *A Good Provider Is One Who Leaves*, Jason DeParle writes about one such family that migrated around the world just for that purpose: to enable their children to have what they needed to thrive.[4] DeParle's book focuses on a family he initially studied several decades ago, learning about the extreme impoverished conditions in the Philippines. A family living in a shantytown outside of Manila let him live with them, and he followed their stories through the years. Tita and Emet and their five children lived in the shantytown for many years, suffering through the stench and crime of their neighborhood, until, finally, Emet had an opportunity to do something different.

In the 1970s, the president of the Philippines began encouraging its citizens to seek employment abroad. The country had too many laborers, and so President Marcos went about setting up contracts with foreign countries that would allow Filipinos to work overseas. Emet saw other men going to Saudi Arabia on contracts to work, bringing home money for their families who now could afford new roofs and education for their children. Emet saw what these men could do, and compared it to the $2.40 he was making a day cleaning swimming pools and selling food on the streets. His boss told him about an opportunity to clean pools for a fitness facility in Dhahran, Saudi Arabia. His salary would rise to $500 a month. He could not pass it up. Emet left his family in the Philippines to clean pools in Dhahran for two years.

With Emet gone and sending home money, Tita raised their five kids and used the money for food, uniforms, and a rare commodity: a toilet. In their shantytown, they were now the proud owners of one of the few toilets in the community. And yet, even with this improvement, they still lived in a shanty. Life was still hard, even with the extra income being sent in from overseas.

One of those children noticed the fine pressed linens worn by the nurses at the nearby nursing school, and her aspirations grew until she was able to attend as a student herself. Her name was Rosalie, and becoming a nurse opened a door to another world. After working hard to make it through nursing school in the Philippines, Rosalie struggled to find a job. With so many nursing graduates, the hospitals there in the Philippines had no shortage. Eventually, an uncle who had left to work in Saudi Arabia came home and told her about a hospital recruiting nurses. So at the age of twenty-five years old, Rosalie took a job thousands of miles away, as her father had, in a hospital outside of Mecca in Saudi Arabia, where she could make $375 a month. After working there for several years on a contract, she met a Filipino man also working there on contract. The two of them flew home to the Philippines to wed, and soon thereafter Rosalie became pregnant with their first child. The two returned to Saudi Arabia to work until the baby was born. Rosalie flew back to deliver the baby around her family. Her mother Tita and older sister Rowena were there to help her in the early months. But then, Rosalie had to choose: stay at home in the Philippines, away from her husband, or return to work to support the family. With her daughter only seven months old, Rosalie flew back to the Middle East, leaving her baby in the care of her mother and sister.

Rosalie may strike us as an unusual mother, leaving her child behind in the Philippines while she worked halfway around the world. And yet, she is also a parent trying to do what she can so that her children can succeed and thrive. She had to spend many years away from her children while working abroad in the Middle East, but her goal was to make it to the United States. A nursing agency that had recruited her from the Philippines would be able to connect her to a hospital in America, but first she had to pass her English exam and get a visa. Moving to the United States would enable her to reunite with her children as she would be able to bring them with her. After seven years of work in the Middle East, Rosalie was able to move to Galveston, Texas, with her husband and their three kids.

In American schools, their three elementary-aged children struggled with their English and fitting in. But after three years, each one had made significant progress and seemed to be thriving. Rosalie had purchased a new home in a housing development farther away from the hospital, but in the same cul-de-sac as other Filipino immigrants, making the place feel like home. The family returned to visit the Philippines when Rosalie's father became sick, and the mother and father who had worked so hard for their five children were able to see their daughter and grandchildren and how they were thriving.

Rosalie was born in a shanty on the other side of the world, and now she is raising her children in a cul-de-sac and working as a nurse in a hospital in Texas. Jason DeParle's retelling of their story covers the struggles as well as the successes—the stress and homesickness Rosalie encountered while living abroad, missing her children, as well as the improvements to the lives of everyone in their extended family as a result of these employment opportunities.

Rosalie's cousin and her husband had another story of trying to live into the dream of providing for their family. Manu and Ariane both worked on cruise ships. The Philippines is one of the primary places from which cruise ships employ their workers. For a Filipino to get a job working as a maid on a cruise ship meant significant financial resources for her family back in the Philippines. Manu also worked on the ships as a laborer who would help with the docking—very dangerous work. One day, one of the ropes snapped while Manu was on the crew docking the ship, and the rope hit him so hard in the back of the leg that it injured him. A crushed artery led to a clot, which went undiagnosed by the ship doctor. Eventually, they got Manu to a hospital in the United States where doctors had to cut off his leg below the knee, and then eventually also above his knee. Manu would not be able to work on cruise ships again and had to return to the Philippines. Luckily, he was able to spend time with his children, while his wife, Ariane, still worked aboard ships and sent money home. But the experience was very difficult, and Manu had been close to losing his life.

What are the risks parents take to provide for their families? To make a decent living wage? Rosalie worked for years in a foreign country, sending back money to support her children and extended family. Her father had worked abroad before her, cleaning pools in Saudi Arabia. Manu and Ariane worked on cruise ships, often risking their own physical safety. And yet, the financial pay-off for these families often seemed to be worth the risk.

Families portrayed in the studies presented by Robert Putnam in *Our Kids* show that financial support can greatly increase a child's opportunities for success. Parents today are often struggling to succeed themselves, and when they lose their jobs or access to a steady income, they may not be able to be supportive of their own children. Here is where the title of Putnam's book comes in: stressing the "our" in *Our Kids*. When we as a society see *all* children as *ours*, we can work to provide more opportunities for children who are not our own.

The story of Rachel and Leah in Genesis at the surface appears to be two women fighting over a man's love and trying to set themselves apart as significant and worthy. But looking at the biblical context means understanding the forces at play that limited their options: the deceit of their father and the cruel cultural norms that insisted a woman's worth rested on how many children she could have. Reading the text *with* these women means listening to these larger cultural forces that led them to feel they needed to compete with one another, rather than support each other.

Much of parenting today is also a struggle for significance, trying to enable our children to have opportunities that we ourselves may not have had. Many parents feel a scarcity of opportunities; aware of elite colleges' rates of admission and a tough job market, many parents feel the need to compete against one another for a limited set of opportunities available to our children. But looking at the larger cultural context, there are forces working against many parents and children that prevent them from having these same opportunities available to them. What if instead of pitting us against one another, parenting drew us together as a common human family? What if raising our own children also made us more aware of the needs of other families who do not have the same resources as we do? What might we do to better support other families?

What would it look like if we were to imaginatively go back and support Rachel and Leah? If instead of shaking our heads at their back-and-forth rivalry, we empathized with their struggles and offered to help in some way? What might that look like?

What would it look like today to help parents who are struggling to give their kids the same opportunities that many wealthy families take for granted? Rather than families fighting over the best spot in choice schools, what would it take for them to put that energy into making more schools successful, and hence more students and families successful? Does the success of one family necessarily come at the expense of others? Or can it, as in the case of Rosalie's family, expand into the well-being of others in the community?

Questions for Reflection

1. In reading the story of Rachel and Leah through the lens of competitive parenting, what do you see as the major fears at stake for these women?

2. In considering modern forms of competitive parenting, what are the fears at stake for families today?

3. What does it look like to be a "good mom" or a "good dad"? What are the pressures you face to live up to such an image?

4. What would cooperative parenting look like in your neighborhood? How might your church participate in supporting such collaborative efforts?

5. Thinking about Rosalie's story, are there other examples of families you know who have had to actually be distant from their children in order to provide for them? What are the challenges they have faced in making that arrangement work? What are the benefits?

6. How do you see families making it work today in ways that do not always look like the traditional "good mom" or "good dad" style of parenting? Where do you see collaborative models of parenting at work?

7. Where do you see God in our struggles to parent our children? When have you felt God's presence as you have felt your own inadequacies as a parent?

Chapter 9

Reconciling with Your Siblings as an Adult

SCRIPTURE: GENESIS 25:19–34 (THE TWINS' BIRTH AND BIRTHRIGHT);
GENESIS 27:1–45 (THE THEFT OF THE BLESSING); GENESIS 32:22–32
(THE WRESTLING MATCH); GENESIS 33:1–17 (REUNION AND SEPARATION)[1]

Introduction

The relationship between Jacob, the patriarch of Israel, and his twin brother Esau, as with many of our own relationships to family members, is complex and fraught. Pockmarked with instances of betrayal, deception, manipulation, and rivalry, the rich stories of these twin brothers, both of whom will become the founder of neighboring ancient Near Eastern nations, Edom and Israel, speak of deep childhood and intrafamilial wounds. Such wounds might be familiar to many of us with regard to our own family. In the narratives about this particular relationship, however, the initial contentious and competitive relationship between the brothers comes to a generally satisfactory conclusion as the twins, after having undergone life-changing experiences, meet again as adults and are able to reconcile. Though it is unclear whether the two will ever come to trust each other fully, their story of initial strife and later rapprochement offers hope of similar reconciliation of wounds and grievances in our own families.

Rebekah's Twins

Before we get to the détente between the brothers, we must begin with the origins of their discord and rivalry. Jacob and Esau's story begins in Genesis 25 with the infertility of their mother, Rebekah, wife of the patriarch Isaac, who, like many of Israel's matriarchs, has trouble conceiving. Unlike them, however, Rebekah's infertility is rapidly resolved as she conceives almost immediately after Isaac prays for her (Gen. 25:21).

The unusually quick resolution does not mean she has an easy pregnancy, however. Rather, the narrative quickly moves to another problem: the tumult caused by her unborn, though surprisingly belligerent children. Her two sons are aggressively fighting—the Hebrew verb used here can be translated as "dashing," "crushing," or "oppressing"—with each other inside her womb. That Rebekah's pregnancy is distressingly painful is evident in her statement in Genesis 25:22, which in Hebrew states literally: "If thus, why this me?"—usually translated as, "If it is to be this way, why do I live?" Rebekah's incoherent statement bespeaks her pain, and therefore, easily intersects with current issues about the pain that women suffer both during and after their pregnancies. Though childbirth is seen as a miraculous and joyful event, it can take a severe physical and mental toll on women and their bodies with some women even experiencing post-traumatic stress disorder as a result of giving birth.[2] This issue speaks to the larger challenges, be they physical or mental, that women shoulder, sometimes silently, especially with regard to the family.

The Oracle about the Twins

Rebekah, instead of suffering in silence, takes matters into her own hand by seeking an oracle from God. There, her difficult pregnancy is explained as the result of twins—twins who are so competitive and bellicose that they cannot even share the same womb without fighting. The oracle explains further that their aggression has larger, international significance as these children will become founders of two different, competing nations (Gen. 25:23).

The oracle in Genesis 25:23 is usually translated as, "the elder shall serve the younger," and therefore as foretelling how Jacob, the younger twin, will be greater than Esau, his slightly older brother. However, good oracles are not usually so straightforward as they can be easily disproven. Take, for example, the famous and ambiguous Delphic oracle to the wealthy ruler, Croesus, that if he crosses the River Halys to battle the Persians, a great empire will fall. The empire that this oracle was referring was not that of the Persians, as Croesus assumed, but his own.

Similarly, the oracle in Genesis 25 is much more cryptic than it first appears. Because of the way that Hebrew works, the oracle can either be stating that "the greater (or bigger) will serve the lesser (or smaller)," *or* that "the lesser (or smaller) will serve the greater (or bigger)." In short, the oracle is unclear both to the identity of the brother—who will be the lesser and who will be the greater?—and also about which one, the greater or lesser, will serve whom. Like all good oracles, this oracle thus leaves the interpretation of the oracle to the reader; and also leaves the fates of the brothers, not simply to destiny or divine will, but to their own choices, decisions, and actions. The twins themselves, through their actions, will determine who will be greater or lesser, and who will serve whom.

The ambiguity of the oracle moreover alludes to the inheritance problem caused by twins. Practically speaking, because twins were born at nearly the same time, not much distinguishes them. One way that ancient stories made sense of this was by depicting twins as rivals—perhaps the most famous of such rivalrous twins are Romulus, the mythic founder of Rome, and his twin, Remus. In the case of Esau and Jacob, their rivalry is heightened because of the Abrahamic promise. Not only will one of these brothers inherit double the possessions of their father and carry on his lineage, but one of them will also become the bearer of the Abrahamic promise.

Considering this competitive setup, it is no wonder that Jacob and Esau are already fighting in the womb. Indeed, their struggle to be the prominent, firstborn child is evident by the way in which the twins exit the womb. Jacob emerges shortly after Esau grasping his brother's heel. Wordplay in the Hebrew elucidates and playfully brings out the rivalry. The word for heel, *'aqev*, sounds a lot like Jacob's name, *ya'aqov*. Moreover, Genesis 25:24–25 describes Esau as red and hairy, which seems odd until we realize that this description of his redness (*'admoni*) and hairiness (*se'ar*) puns with Edom, the country founded by Esau, of which Seir is the major region.

Offenses and Wounds in the Family

Hinting of a larger divide in the family, the text moreover tells us that each twin was favored by one of the parents: Jacob is beloved by his mother (v. 28), while Esau, a hunter, is favored by his meat-loving father. As with Cain and Abel, and also Isaac and Ishmael, parents or parental figures exacerbate the sibling competition by playing favorites.

Adding to contrast, the twins are said to have different, almost oppositional personalities. Esau is described as an outdoorsy hunter, "a man of the field" (v. 27), while his brother, in contrast, is said to be a quiet man, living in tents—an odd description, which the rabbis read as representative of Jacob's scholarly nature. Jacob, we will find out shortly, also likes to cook. Perhaps most importantly, Jacob is depicted as ambitious, tricky, and clever; and rather keen to outsmart his more dimwitted older brother—which he does in two instances.

The first instance is described in Genesis 25:29–34 when Esau comes back hungry from the field, sees Jacob cooking a red stew, and asks if he can have some of "that red red stuff" (Gen. 25:30). Esau's uncouth, almost nonverbal speech makes clear that he is not the brightest bulb. To this request, Jacob uncharitably asks Esau to exchange the stew for Esau's birthright—a ludicrous request considering that the birthright entails double the inheritance. Yet to this unfair exchange Esau quickly agrees, displaying his foolishness, lack of long-term planning, and ultimately his unworthiness to be the bearer of the Abrahamic promise. Jacob, too, is portrayed negatively. Unbrotherly, calculating, and ruthlessly ambitious, he refuses his own brother food unless he first gives away most of his inheritance.

This uncharitable act is followed by a second more egregious act of deception, though we should note that Jacob is not alone in his plot. Genesis 27 tells of how Isaac, who is now blind and perhaps on his deathbed, asks Esau to get him some game so that he can eat it and give him the blessing meant for the firstborn. While Esau is away hunting, Esau's own mother, Rebekah, urges and helps Jacob thieve the blessing by dressing up as the hairy Esau in goat skin. That this ploy is outrageous and reprehensible, even by Jacob's low standards, is confirmed by Jacob, who tells his mother that he is worried that he might be discovered and cursed by his father instead. Rebekah, however, reassures her son, even promising to take on any curse if their trick is discovered (Gen. 27:13). As we will see, though mother and son ultimately get away with this plot, both will pay a price at the end.

Despite some initial hesitation by Isaac (27:21–22), Jacob succeeds in his ruse, leading some interpreters to wonder whether Isaac was willingly playing along with it or even whether God "blinded" Isaac's senses so that God's favored person can receive the blessing meant for his undeserving brother. These interpretations rightly highlight the dysfunctionality of the first family of Israel—of which God was a member. And in so doing, these unfavorable stories of Israel's ancestor provide a rich and messy window into the complicated nature of all families. The biblical writers do not sugarcoat things but instead, through their writings, reflect upon the complexities of the family and the ways in which our destructive actions can have lasting and tragic consequences on the family unit.

Indeed, for these familial "crimes," some of the characters do pay some kind of price. Jacob, as we saw in a previous chapter, is forced to marry

both of his cousins, Leah and Rachel, who engage in a similar competition of their own (Gen. 29–30). Moreover, Jacob continues to favor some
of his children over others to the great detriment of his favorite son,
Joseph, who is sold as a slave by his jealous brothers and ends up exiled in
Egypt. Jacob therefore loses his favorite son—indeed, father and son are
separated for most of their lives—and the family of Israel is nearly permanently fractured as a result of Jacob's favoritism (Gen. 37–50).

Rebekah too might have paid a price for her favoritism. As a result
of the theft of the blessing, Esau is so angry that he plans to kill Jacob,
thereby almost replaying the Cain and Abel story (27:41). As a result,
Rebekah advises Jacob to relocate to her brother's house in order to wait
out Esau's fury. She tells him that when Esau's anger has died down, she
will send for Jacob so that he can return. Yet this is not what happens. As
we discussed in the previous chapter, Jacob will go to his uncle, Laban,
and will end up marrying his two cousins. He will never again see his
mother. For all of Rebekah's deception of her family members to help
her favored child get ahead, she will be rewarded with the loss of that
favorite child as Jacob moves away never to be reunited with her.

The Wrestling Match

Though Jacob never again sees his parents after his move to his uncle's
house, he does, however, reunite with his brother Esau long enough to
rectify their fractured relationship somewhat. By Genesis 31, Jacob and
his now rather large family consisting of four wives and numerous children (and also servants and slaves) decide to return to Canaan. In order
to get there, however, Jacob and his family have to journey through territory belonging to Esau, that is, the territory of Edom, something which
Jacob, understandably, is not very keen on.

A different life situation adds to Jacob's distress. When Jacob originally fled his father's house, he had little to lose. Now, as a patriarch with
a large family and lots of stuff, he has much to lose—and also much to
think about. That Jacob is internally struggling and even reassessing his
previous behavior is evident by a strange predawn wrestling match that
Jacob has with a mysterious figure before his reunion with Esau (Gen.
32:24–32). During the struggle, Jacob is not only touched on the hip
bone, dislocating it, but he, like Abraham and Sarah, is given a new name:
Israel. The name, the real meaning of which remains a mystery, is given a
false explanation as having something to do with Jacob's predawn struggle: "Then the man said, 'You shall no longer be called Jacob, but Israel,

for you have striven with God and with humans, and have prevailed'"
(Gen. 32:28). Indeed, imbedded in the name "Israel" are sounds that are
phonetically akin to the Hebrew word *sarah*, which means "to strive," "to
contend with," and "to persevere."

Jacob's new name fits with the themes of striving and struggling that
run throughout the stories we have explored. Jacob's life indeed is a series
of struggles: He fights with his brother both in and out of the womb,
clashes with Laban, his uncle, for wife and property, and now he tussles
with a mysterious being who renames him before his reunion with his
brother. Not just Jacob, but, as evident by the numerous tales of sibling
competition and parental favoritism in Genesis, struggle defines almost
all of the relationships of the members of the first families of Israel. It
is fitting therefore that Jacob's new name is the same one as that of the
nation that will claim descent from him. The name, Israel, if it is related
to the word "to strive," embodies the struggles, difficulties, and pain that
mark Jacob's family and the family of Israel as a whole.

That the story of Jacob's wrestling match concerns intrafamilial struggles is evident not only by the name change, but also from the context of
the story. This struggle occurs right before his reunion with his brother
Esau. Indeed, some interpreters have wondered whether Jacob's wrestling partner is not really some divine being, but actually his twin. This
idea finds some support in an odd statement that Jacob makes. After
the struggle is over, Jacob marks and names the place of the predawn
wrestling match, Peniel, because, as he explains, "I have seen God face
to face. . . ." (32:30). This phrase sounds eerily similar to what Jacob says
to Esau when they are reunited. When Jacob sees Esau, he tells him that
seeing his face "is like seeing the face of God" (33:10). Is God or the
divine wrestling partner used as a stand-in for Esau in this tale? And if so,
is this story hinting that the brothers had a pre-union fight where they
hashed out—physically—their previous grievances between themselves?
If so, this would explain why their reunion is so surprisingly amicable
and peaceful.

Regardless of the true identity of Jacob's wrestling partner, his statement to Esau—that seeing him is like seeing the face of *God*—hints that
intrafamilial struggles are envisioned by the biblical writers as intimately
related to God and, hence, of theological significance. As evident by the
stories we have explored, God, especially because of God's promises
to Abraham, is intimately involved with the family of Israel and their
struggles and issues. If so, then as we move from text to the world, these
biblical narratives suggest that not only is God present in the midst of

our family issues and situations, but that we need to reimagine struggles within the family as also theologically meaningful and relevant.

Other interpretations of Jacob's predawn wrestling match also suggest that family issues are theologically significant. Some interpreters maintain that this fight was not really something real or physical, but something that took place in Jacob's head. The struggle, according to this interpretation, reflects the mental or psychological struggle that Jacob was undergoing before his reunion with his brother—the brother whom he had wronged and taken advantage of. Left alone in the dark, Jacob is left alone with his thoughts. Perhaps he is thinking about his past, his relationships with his family members, and in particular, his treatment of his brother, Esau, who he is about to see again in the morning. Twisting and turning, perhaps he is going over what has happened, what he had done, and what will happen to him and his family in the not so distant future. Perhaps that's why Jacob tells Esau that seeing him is like seeing the face of God. About to come face to face with his brother, his twin and his oppositional other, Jacob is psychologically confronted with his past, present, and future, and all the familial misdeeds in which he participated.

Perhaps the writers envisioned this psychological reflection as a kind of physical struggle with a divine being—a struggle from which Jacob emerged wounded yet transformed. That Jacob is changed by the struggle, be it physically or mentally, is supported by the new name given to Jacob by his wrestling partner (32:28). Names in the biblical text are not just arbitrary designations but signify something real and essential about a particular person or being. If so, then Jacob, based on the new name, has changed in some fundamental way. If the new name, Israel, is related to the word *sarah*, as the text suggests, Jacob's new name therefore reflects both his past struggles and striving, much of which centered on his family, and also his perseverance and ability to overcome them (32:28). According to his new name, Jacob and the community of people that will emerge from him will be marked not only by their intrafamilial struggles but also by their ability to survive, to live through the struggle, and maybe to come out the other side damaged (Jacob, after all, retains a permanent limp because of the fight), but transformed.

The Reconciliation of Jacob and Esau

After this predawn wrestling match, the brothers finally are reunited. The scene in Genesis 33 begins rather forebodingly, with Jacob seeing Esau approaching him from afar with four hundred men. Fearful that Esau is about to attack, Jacob organizes his group by placing those he cares the most about—Rachel and Joseph—in the very back (33:2). Like so many of us, despite a life-changing event (the wrestling match), Jacob's more troubling predilection for favoritism remains. His family appropriately organized, Jacob approaches Esau warily, bowing to his brother seven times. Jacob has already prepared for his meeting by sending Esau a series of presents beforehand (32:13–20). His humble manner of approach, albeit done out of fear, might hint that Jacob has, however, learned some lessons. Here he is sending gifts and bowing seven times to a sibling who he has spent his entire life trying to trick and steal from. One even wonders if the obscure oracle—either the lesser or the greater will serve the other—alludes to this instance of Jacob's supplication to Esau when they are briefly reunited.

Indeed, it is not just Jacob who appears to have changed and grown up as this scene of initial dread transforms into one of heartwarming reunion and reconciliation: "But Esau ran to meet him, and embraced him, and fell on his neck and kissed him, and they wept" (Gen. 33:4). The string of verbs captures the heightened emotions of this reunion. Esau and Jacob are genuinely happy to see each other, as they embrace and weep together—this is a wrestling match without any violence or contention. Esau is eager to meet his brother's large family, and both brothers seem glad that things have turned out well for the other (Gen. 33:5–7). By all appearances, therefore, it seems that Esau has forgiven his brother for his past offenses. If so, then this narrative suggests that reconciliation and recovery from childhood wounds are indeed possible.

Reconciliation and healing, however, is a process and not an event. In some situations, reconciliation with family members might be impossible because it can lead to more psychological damage or a repetition of trauma. Indeed, we might have fractured relationships with some family members who are unready or unwilling to mend them. The complex process of healing, especially of familial wounds, is also hinted at in this story. The brothers' reunion is very brief, and as soon as they meet, Jacob seems eager to depart and go on his way. Hinting of lingering distrust, Jacob declines Esau's request to travel together throughout Esau's lands with an excuse (33:12–17). Moreover, when Esau suggests that he leave some of his men with Jacob's family so that they can transverse the land safely, Jacob again refuses (33:15). It seems that Jacob is still wary and distrustful of his brother. Perhaps he thinks that Esau is looking for a way to attack him and his family in the future. Perhaps the text is even insinuating that Esau has not fully forgiven his brother, and that Esau, as Jacob suspects, is waiting until Jacob's guard is down to take his revenge. Certainly, if Jacob and Esau reflect the nations of which they are progenitors—Israel and Edom—this lingering disquiet makes sense as the relationship between the two nations will prove to be deeply ambivalent.

Ambivalent Reconciliation

The story of Esau and Jacob with its ambivalent reconciliation embodies our discussion of families in Genesis: both the hope of transformation, healing, and reconciliation within our families; and also the lengthy, perhaps lifelong process they sometimes require. After all, relationships as well as individuals in families do not remain fixed. We see this in the story of Jacob and Esau as they move from a fractured relationship of rivalry, competition, and parental favoritism toward one of reconciliation, mutual joy, and healing. The reconciliation, however, remains ambivalent at the end, as is the case in many families. This is unsurprising considering that families are as complex and shifting as the people and other creatures who compose them.

Reconciling Jacob and Esau, Reconciling Siblings Today

The story of Jacob and Esau makes it hard to root for Jacob. Though he is the patriarch in the triad of patriarchs mentioned in the Bible, when it refers to God as the God of "Abraham, Isaac, and Jacob," he may not be the typical hero we want to look up to. He tricks his brother, lies to his father, and gets away with his father's blessing that should have gone to Esau. If we took the side of Esau in this story, we would rightfully be bitter and upset.

Are there sibling relationships that you know of that are equally combative? Siblings who fought over a parent's will? Or siblings who said or did such hurtful things to one another that they are no longer on speaking terms? I know a few examples, unfortunately. Sibling relationships can be challenging. Children can feel—even as adults—as though they are competing for their parents' love and attention, especially when it comes to how that love is monetized in the form of an inheritance.

One woman shared with me the story of their aging mother who lived in another town. One sister lived with her for a time, but then had to relocate because of her own family. Then their brother moved in with the mother. The elderly mother was coming down with dementia, and the son insisted that she transfer all of her accounts into his name so that he could make sure all the bills were paid on time. The woman telling me the story said that her brother then proceeded to take money out of their mother's account, including buying himself a new truck. The son eventually put their mother in a nursing home and sold her house, without telling his sisters and without distributing any of the funds from the sale of the house to the sisters. What upset this woman the most about her brother's actions was that he got rid of all of the family photographs that were in their mother's house.

Stories told about siblings are typically only told from one point of view; it is hard to get siblings together to have each share their side of the story. I do not know the side of the brother, just the side of the woman telling me the story. But is there any hope of reconciliation between these siblings? It is hard to know.

The source of Jacob and Esau's discord was their fight over their father's blessing and Esau's birthright. To consider these elements today, we might think about what parents bequeath to their children in a will. If the parents decide not to distribute their financial assets equally, or if the children sense that the assets are being distributed unequally, then disagreements and fighting can ensue, including litigation. Siblings will take each other to court to sue one another over their parents' will. If siblings have thus divided the "birthright" and have fought over who got more of what they perceived to be theirs, what is left of the relationship? Is there any way to reconcile? It is hard to know.

Adult siblings can become divided over any number of issues, including political views or different opinions over how to take care of aging parents. When siblings do not see eye to eye, it may be easy for them to stay away from one another, living in different parts of the country, focusing on their own immediate families, or simply avoiding one another around town. It may be that a sibling has a mental illness, and their personality is hard to get along with, and so the other siblings tend to stay away.

As we have discussed in earlier chapters, these biblical passages and stories about families do not so much tell us how to act or behave as give us an example of the struggles families can face. The ancient world had its share of dysfunctional families, as do we today. And yet, is there something we can learn from Jacob and Esau coming back together and reuniting, albeit briefly, in this passage? Is there something we can take from their story that can help us navigate the sibling struggles that adults today may encounter?

Adult Siblings and the Gift Exchange

One possible takeaway is the image of a gift exchange. Ahead of meeting his brother, Jacob sends on to Esau a series of gifts. It may be that he was hoping these gifts would soften his brother's anger. In return, Esau meets Jacob with a surprising gift: a joyous reception, running to meet him and falling on his neck and weeping. This encounter seems so extraordinary; Esau's reception of his trickster brother is so surprisingly full of grace and forgiveness, that we should read it as a special gift.

Adult siblings, even those estranged from one another, may at times give one another gifts. Perhaps at holidays or birthdays, a sibling may send a gift or a brief greeting. Perhaps there is a tradition among the families of exchanging gifts for the next generation, and so adult siblings get gifts for their nieces and nephews. Or it may be that adult siblings no longer exchange gifts, let alone contact one another around the holidays or birthdays; perhaps they are too estranged even for that level of contact. But what if that practice were to be started up again, just by one of the siblings? What might that accomplish?

French sociologist Marcel Mauss wrote a brief essay titled *The Gift*, originally published in French in 1925 and later translated into English in 1954.[3] His reflections influenced philosophers like Jacques Derrida and Paul Ricoeur. His writing looked at the gift-giving practices of some societies, and suggested that the practice of the gift exchange could be beneficial as a social model for group interaction. That is, rather than focusing on transactions made purely for money or consumption, the gift exchange as a social practice pointed to human capacities of generosity and altruism. In his book *The Course of Recognition*, Paul Ricoeur draws from this idea to consider how political struggles for recognition could be reimagined in this way as an opportunity for a gift exchange.[4] The words we use shape the way we think; and if we are fighting for recognition, then our reality will often be one of conflict. If instead we are offering gifts to others in an exchange, then the way we perceive our efforts will feel distinctly different.

In terms of relating to siblings, could estranged adults be able to reconnect as persons exchanging gifts? It may seem unlikely, especially when there has been significant conflict in the relationship in the past. When one sibling has cheated the family or been dishonest, it can be hard to trust that the gift comes with no strings attached.

The story of Jacob and Esau is exactly such a story of conflict; and yet, the gift exchange succeeded. It may not have been Jacob's gifts that won Esau over, but Esau himself offered a gift of himself, warmly greeting his brother and offering to assist him through the country. The gift exchange completed, we can imagine the two brothers able to go their separate ways in peace.

Could adults today practice the same kind of gift exchange and hope for the same results in their relationships with estranged siblings? It is hard to know. One way to test this theory is to put it into practice.

Siblings Gathered Together

My (Carolyn) mom's sister hosted a family reunion this past summer. Three of the four siblings of that generation came together, along with their children and grandchildren. My aunt also invited her cousins to join the family reunion, reconnecting with the children of her parents' siblings. It was one big happy family, in the best sense.

One of the things I admired about my mother and her siblings was the way they got together before the death of their parents. When my grandparents had to sell their home before moving into assisted living, their children all gathered together and went through the house with stickers, identifying the items they wanted for themselves or their children. Together they laughed and they cried, mourning what they knew was coming. My grandparents died five years apart, and both of their funerals seemed like big family reunions. My mother and her siblings all seem to get along together so well, even though they had their differences. There were definitely moments of conflict over the years, but nothing that prevented them from getting together on a regular basis.

Perhaps in your family, too, over the years, there have been sources of conflict. Even if you do not have a feuding Jacob and Esau, there may be plenty of family drama. And yet, with the passage of time and the grace learned from making our own mistakes, hopefully we can all come to the awareness of the gift that is present to us in family, including the gift of lessons we learn about ourselves and one another along the way.

Questions for Reflection

1. If you have adult siblings from whom you are estranged, can you practice some form of gift exchange? What might that look like? What could you possibly hope to gain from the experience?
2. What are the benefits to siblings who support one another into adulthood? If you have siblings you are on good terms with, what are the benefits you see to your relationship?

3. If you had advice to give other adults who are struggling with sibling relationships, what might you encourage them to do?
4. Have you seen positive examples of adult siblings staying in relationship with one another? What are some of the practices that you see them doing that help them maintain those relationships?
5. Esau's response to Jacob seems full of grace and forgiveness; is there a time when you have experienced that coming from someone else? Have you been able to express that toward someone who has wronged you in the past? Has it felt in any way like a gift, both to offer that grace and to release that past hurt?
6. What can Jacob and Esau's brief reconciliation help us imagine for the divisions in the church? In society?
7. If there was one thing you would want to say to a sister or brother, what would it be?

Chapter 10

A Death in the Family

SCRIPTURE: GENESIS 23:1–24:67; GENESIS 35:16–20

Introduction

When a family member dies, that family is irrevocably changed. Despite mentioning the deaths of major characters, the biblical text is typically reticent about the details of a character's death, most notably the sense of loss that other characters have in their absence. This does not mean that the deaths of particular people do not affect the family unit or the other members of the family, however. Rather, the silence of the text urges the reader to interrogate the stories more carefully in order to discover the ways in which the loss of a family member reverberates in the stories of those characters who are left behind.

The Death of Sarah

Sarah's death, to some degree, should not come as much of a surprise. Already advanced in her years when we meet her and her husband, Abraham, in Genesis 12, she is 127 years old when she dies (Gen. 23:1–2). Yet despite our awareness of her age, her death still seems rather sudden. There is no buildup, no hint of her coming demise. No mention of sickness, no hint of weakness. Rather, the story summarily proceeds from telling us that Abraham has tried to kill his son (Gen. 22) to informing us in the next chapter that Sarah had died (Gen. 23:2). So sudden is the jump that, as was noted previously, some interpreters link the two events, suggesting that Sarah's death resulted from her discovery of her husband's failed attempt at filicide.

The unexpected nature of Sarah's death likely resonates with many of us. It might be that the death of anyone close to us, no matter how old or what the circumstances, seems sudden and unexpected. Though we realize that everyone gets older and that the next day is not guaranteed, there are some people who are so crucial, so necessary to us and our place in this world, that their death, even if they are sick, still catches us unaware, and feels sudden, too soon. In light of the 2020 worldwide COVID-19 pandemic, many readers, unfortunately, can likely empathize with this feeling of shock that comes from the suddenness of death and the emptiness it can leave behind.

Despite the suddenness of Sarah's death, the biblical text is less open about the ramifications of her demise, thereby forcing us to draw our own conclusions from hints and silences. Rather than speaking directly to Abraham's grief, the text recounts in several verses how Abraham purchased the field of Ephron in Machpelah as a family burial plot (23:3–20), and his decision to start looking for a wife for Isaac (Gen. 24). Perhaps in detailing the logistics of the burial, the biblical text reflects both the mundane arrangements that must take place, and the cold comfort these actions can provide. In this reading, Abraham's actions might also speak to a kind of despair, sadness, or numbness that he feels: Losing his spouse of many decades, maybe he is just trying to keep busy. Perhaps too the burden of masculine expectation prevents the patriarch from expressing his emotions out loud: Better to take care of tasks than to weep and moan.

Turning to Isaac, we can see that Sarah's son feels the loss of his mother acutely and that he might have trouble expressing those emotions, like his father. Considering how much Sarah cared for and protected Isaac, it seems likely that her death would have deeply affected him. Sarah, after all, was the one who swiftly worked to remove Isaac's half brother, Ishmael, because he posed a threat to Isaac's inheritance. Likewise, Sarah's explanations of Isaac's name as meaning "laughter" hint of her happiness and joy over the birth of her son (21:6).

As with his father, however, the text is generally silent as to Isaac's feelings. Indeed, Isaac seems to have inherited a trait of poor communication from Abraham with whom he barely speaks. Part of this might stem from his father's attempt to kill him (Gen. 22), which would surely have put a damper on the relationship, though it is still noteworthy that the two are rarely depicted talking with each other. Indeed, the only time they converse is the story of Isaac's sacrifice (Gen. 22) when Isaac, either innocently or suspiciously, asks his father about the whereabouts of the sacrificial lamb. It shouldn't surprise us, then, when Isaac never mentions his mother's death, either to Abraham or anyone else: He has evidently suppressed his grief and cannot discuss it.

Despite Isaac's reticence, however, the text hints at the deep sadness of this character. This is apparent in the events leading up to his marriage with Rebekah. First, in the search for a wife, he is unusual. For some reason, Isaac not only fails to go out and find his own spouse, like his son Jacob does, but, as Genesis 24:5–8 shows, his father seems almost terrified of letting Isaac out of his sight. Is this overprotectiveness due to Abraham having recently lost his spouse, or because Isaac, after Ishmael's forced exit, is the only remaining heir to the Abrahamic promise? Perhaps the hesitation has to do with the son. Is Isaac still traumatized over his father's attempt to kill him, or is he depressed and still trying to process the death of his mother and is not up to task of looking for a spouse so soon? Some interpreters have even posited that Isaac has some sort of physical or mental impairment, which might have limited his ability to find a match.

Whatever the reason, Isaac remains at home while his future spouse, Rebekah, is brought to him. And it is when he encounters and marries Rebekah that we, the readers, finally get a sense of how deeply affected he was by the death of his mother and how his wife will begin to salve the loss of his mother in a manner suggestive of Sarah herself. Straightaway, the meeting of Rebekah and Isaac hints that Isaac's dark cloud over his mother's death might be beginning to lift. Genesis 24:63–66 states that when Isaac is out walking one evening, he sees a caravan approaching. When Rebekah, who is part of the caravan, catches sight of Isaac, she stumbles from the saddle.

This initially seems like a strange and somewhat comical introduction, but one interpretation brings out the particularly riotous and borderline obscene humor of these events. The word used to describe what Isaac is doing in the field is difficult to translate, but one possible meaning is to defecate or urinate. Thus the reader is left laughing at what is probably the strangest introduction in the Bible: Isaac, out using the bathroom in the field, is suddenly met by his future wife who is so shocked she falls off her camel.[1] This *Three Stooges* moment suggests the happiness and joy that will begin to emerge from the pairing of Isaac and Rebekah. Indeed, as befitting the name Sarah gave him, Isaac, laughter bubbles up from the very moment he meets Rebekah.

The marriage of the two further reinforces the absence of Sarah and the consolation Isaac finds in Rebekah in the face of his loss. The final verse of Genesis 24 states: "Then Isaac brought her into his mother

Sarah's tent. He took Rebekah, and she became his wife; and he loved her. *So Isaac was comforted after his mother's death*" (v. 67; italics added). This last phrase about how Isaac finds comfort by marrying Rebekah is telling as it indicates his state of mind before his marriage—that he was not comforted but deeply grieved or depressed or even barely able to do anything—because of his mom's death. In this little note we see all the emotions and love that Isaac felt for his mother, and, as such, all the ways that her death has changed and will change his life going forward.

The Death of Rachel

Though distressing, Sarah's death is nothing compared to the tragedy and horror of the death of Rachel, the wife of Jacob. On the family's way back to Canaan, Rachel goes into labor. The pain and distress she feels from the difficult birth is evident by the first name that she gives her newly born child as she is dying, Ben-oni, which means "son of my pain or sorrow" (Gen. 35:18). Jacob, her husband, understandably later changes this name to Benjamin, which means "son of the right." Like so many women in the ancient world and still in our own, Rachel dies while giving birth. That Rachel dies in childbirth when her story has centered so long on her infertility and her desire to have children, especially in her competition with her sister, Leah, adds to the tragedy.

Rachel's death appears to have affected the family in rather dramatic ways, leading to loss, conflict, and suffering. First, as we mentioned earlier, after Rachel's death, we never again hear from or about her sister except for one passing mention that Leah was buried (Gen. 49:31). Despite their competitive relationship, it seems that once Rachel dies, so does Leah. Equally affected if not more so is Jacob, Rachel's husband. Rachel is not only Jacob's favorite wife, but, as interpreters have noted, both are depicted as active and tricky, and therefore very similar. In losing Rachel, Jacob thus seems to have lost his other half. The loss of Rachel likely is also the reason why Jacob so favors Joseph, Rachel's first son, even going so far as to give Joseph a coat (37:3–4), which acts to inflame the hatred and jealousy of his other brothers.

This would have long-lasting consequences that would change the trajectory of Jacob's family as well as the nation of Israel. Because of their jealousy, the brothers would sell Joseph into slavery and lie to their father by showing him Joseph's bloodied coat that Joseph had died. As before with parental favoritism, Jacob's favoritism thus leads to a separation from his beloved son for much of their lives. This act of brotherly betrayal would lead to Joseph ending up in Egypt where, after many ups and downs, he would rise to become vizier. Many years later, when the family is reunited, Jacob's entire family will relocate to Egypt, remaining there until Moses is sent to lead them back to Canaan as is described in Exodus.

One wonders whether things would have been different had Rachel lived. Maybe she, like Sarah, would have defended Joseph from his brothers and prevented him from being sold into slavery. Perhaps she would have helped Joseph to be less arrogant or unaware as he is when we first meet him, guilelessly telling his whole family about his dreams, which foretell his coming greatness (37:5–11). Or maybe if Rachel had not died, Jacob would not have so openly favored Rachel's son Joseph, and later, her son Benjamin, which would have improved the relationship among all the siblings.

As Rachel's death shows, a death has the potential to change irrevocably the community of which the person is a part. Though deaths cannot be undone, the biblical text suggests the profound impact that a deceased individual can continue to have: Even in death our family members are not fully gone but still with us somehow. Despite Rachel's death in Genesis 35, this is not the last we see of her in the Bible. Rather, she appears again in Jeremiah 31:15, a verse that is reused in Matthew 2:18, as a weeping and despondent figure watching her children being led into exile. The connection here is important: Exile was seen as akin to death. Unlike when she dies in Genesis 35, however, in Jeremiah, God responds to Rachel, comforting her by promising her that God will bring her children back home. Considering that returning from exile was seen as a kind of revivification or resurrection, God thus reminds Rachel that the deaths of the children of God are not final.

Responding to Death Today

The silences surrounding the deaths of Sarah and Rachel in the biblical text may seem familiar to people who grow up in families that do not talk about death or the dead. The 2019 film *The Farewell* narrates one family's approach to death: keeping the knowledge of their matriarch's cancer a secret from her.[2] The movie stars Awkwafina, who won a Golden Globe for Best Actress, as Billi, a Chinese American who travels with her family back to China to spend time with Nai Nai, her grandmother, who is dying of lung cancer. But Nai Nai's sons, including Billi's father, have forbidden anyone from informing Nai Nai of her condition. Nai Nai's sister takes her to the hospital to get her scans, the sister receives the doctor's information about her condition, and the sister informs her that the doctor has said Nai Nai's lungs have only "benign shadows." Nai Nai's two sons and their families have come to visit her under the auspices of celebrating Billi's cousin's wedding.

Throughout the visit, there is this muted grief among the various members who join with Nai Nai in her loving preparations for the big wedding, while holding inside themselves the heaviness of their sadness. Billi, aware that even the doctors continue to keep the truth from her grandmother, challenges her father and uncle on why they insist on keeping this news from Nai Nai. Shouldn't she know she is dying? Her father and uncle, both clearly upset, tell Billi that it is more important that Nai Nai remains blissfully unaware, and that this is their service to her as her sons: to bear the emotional load for her. Why should she have to carry this weight, when she has done so much for them to make them happy?

The Farewell shows us a beautiful perspective on death and grieving: the power we have to help someone else by sharing the emotional load of grief. In the story of Isaac finding Rebekah, we hear this sense of relief, that here was someone who could help him lighten his load. Without the ability to trust his father following the incident on Mount Moriah, Isaac had no one to confide in, no one to share his grief with, to lessen his pain. With Rebekah, Isaac had someone to comfort him. It is an inspiring message for us, reminding readers today of our ability to come alongside one another in grief. When we ourselves are grieving, we can also find relief in sharing our grief with others who want to help us lighten our load.

But this is only one way of responding to death: There are many others. For some persons, the idea of someone else carrying the burden of grief with you or for you sounds utterly unrealistic. For them, they are the only ones who properly grieve; only they themselves know how much this death meant to them. It is important that we try not to judge others according to some standard of expected grief stages or how we ourselves process loss.

Processing Death as a Community: George Floyd

On Memorial Day 2020, George Floyd was restrained by police, held down on the ground with an officer's knee on his neck. While Floyd called for his mother and cried out "I can't breathe," the officer remained unmoved for a full eight minutes and forty-six seconds. George Floyd died right before our eyes. The video went viral, posted to news feeds and shared around the world, with people responding to his death with fierce protest. Here was a death that millions of people have had to process. For many around the world, it was visual evidence of the long-standing racist treatment of African Americans in the United States, and also an example of the abuse of police power that can be present around the world.

For persons who are not African American, seeing George Floyd's death on video broke through the stories of denial that have served to minimize the complaints of people of color about police brutality. Such stories involve white people blaming the victims, trying to find a reason why the person was detained and had to be killed, looking into the victims' backgrounds for reasons why it was acceptable for this person to die at the hands of police because of some past moral infraction. These stories of justifying deaths are utter cruelty to the loved ones left grieving their loss. And these denials of police brutality cannot be sustained, given the visual evidence provided by video footage of a man held prostrate on the ground by a police officer calmly resting all his weight through his knee on the man's neck, despite the man's frequent cries, "I can't breathe." No story of denial can spin that visual image into something other than it is: a grave injustice.

Persons around the globe responded to George Floyd's death, including Aziz Asmar in war-torn Syria who, with friends, painted a mural to memorialize him.[3] The sense of cruelty and utter lack of empathy in the face of the police officer who knelt on George Floyd's neck spoke to millions of people who have been brutalized by oppressive regimes and unjust social structures. In the United States, protests sprung up around the country as people echoed George Floyd's last words "I can't breathe!" and "Black Lives Matter!," a chant made into a movement following the acquittal of George Zimmerman, who killed unarmed Trayvon Martin. The deaths of unarmed men and women of color have served as rallying cries for all who see systemic racism as a legacy that has never gone away and who want to raise awareness and call attention to ongoing injustice so that others do not have to die prematurely at the hands of the police or fellow citizens.

While the death of George Floyd and others like him have drawn national attention, there are other deaths that we grieve communally, such as when an important public figure passes away. In the same summer as the protests over George Floyd's murder, civil rights icon John Lewis died. People on social media shared memories of how they had come into contact with this esteemed leader and politician who worked tirelessly on civil rights throughout his career. One way we respond to death communally is by sharing our memories of the deceased, telling others the impact the departed has had on our own lives.

Rachel's Death and Maternal Mortality

While some may read of Rachel's death and assume that we have progressed medically to curtail maternal mortality, it is important to read this text while remembering the many women who continue to die in childbirth, including women in the most medically advanced nations in the world. In January 2020, the Centers for Disease Control and Prevention (CDC) released data for the rate of maternal deaths recorded in the year 2018. Due to errors in how this information had been recorded in each state, this was the first year a maternal mortality rate had been released since 2007. In 2018, the mortality rate was 17.4 deaths per every 100,000 women who gave birth.[4] According to the CDC, this translates to approximately 700 women who died in 2018 during pregnancy, at childbirth, or within forty-two days after pregnancy.[5]

The CDC also has a chart showing the steady rise of the rate of maternal mortality over the past three decades.[6] So rather than reducing the number of women who die in pregnancy or childbirth or shortly thereafter, the United States has seen a steady increase in these numbers. And the women who die in childbirth are disproportionately women of color, particularly Black women. For every 100,000 live births or pregnancies of Black mothers, 37.1 Black women die, compared to 14.7 white women per every 100,000 of white women giving birth.[7] Coupled with this racial disparity is the rate of infant mortality: More than twice as many Black infants die (11.4 per 1,000 live births) within the first year after childbirth as white infants (4.9 per 1,000).[8] Researchers are beginning to highlight the racial discrepancies and trying to find reasons for the differences. One suggestion has been that implicit bias operates unconsciously, which means doctors and nurses are less likely to listen to the concerns of Black mothers than white mothers. For example, tennis star Serena Williams made public her experience of having expressed concern about a clot following childbirth that was initially dismissed by her nurses. If she had not persisted in getting a CT scan and the blood thinner she needed, she could have died from the blood clots that had indeed formed in her lungs and at the location of her C-section incision.[9]

As we consider Rachel's death in childbirth, we may not be surprised by her death because women in the Bible did not have access to our current hospitals and advanced medical care. But as we have seen in the statistics from the CDC, women today, even living within the United States, are not protected from dying due to the complications of childbirth. And because of other factors impacting women's health, such as racial discrimination, poverty, and limited access to health care in rural communities, women who give birth continue to face death at the point of bringing into the world a new life.

Death in the Family: Remembered by God

Whose death have you experienced? Whether you have lost a parent, as Isaac lost his mother Sarah, or a spouse, as Jacob lost his wife Rachel in childbirth (and by her absence in the narrative, perhaps losing Leah as well), a death in the family takes a serious toll. The pain can be immense, whether watching someone die over the course of years in the case of illness, or out of nowhere in situations of unforeseen medical emergencies or violent deaths. Death can leave us inconsolable. But as many pastors say over children's heads in baptism, quoting Romans 14:8, "whether we live or whether we die, we are the Lord's." We belong to God in life and in death, and as we see in the stories of these matriarchs from long ago, even in death we are remembered and held dear. Our loved ones who die have been brought into the re-membering arms of God, who brings us together as the body of Christ, uniting us even in the midst of our sorrow.

So too, as we face injustice in the world today, and as we work against oppressions of all kind, we know that while it may take a long time for justice to be fully realized, we continue to be held by God. Breonna Taylor was a young Black woman and emergency medical technician who was killed in her apartment by police officers who entered her home in the middle of the night through a "no-knock" warrant. Believing that someone was breaking in and not knowing that it was the police, her boyfriend fired his gun in self-defense and wounded one of the officers. In response, the police fired off a volley of shots, killing Breonna Taylor. As of this writing in July of 2020, no one associated with her death has been indicted, several months after her killing.[10] As national attention focused on the deaths of unarmed Black men like Ahmaud Arbery and George Floyd in the spring of 2020, many people were also calling out the absence of concern for Breonna Taylor. As has unfortunately been the case, the deaths of women of color have gained less attention than the deaths of men. And yet, in faith, we trust that there is a God who never forgets. The God of our sister Breonna Taylor has never forgotten her, since God created her in God's very image and now holds her close in death.

As children of God, joined together as a family with all of the human race, we trust that God never forgets a single one of God's children who dies. Each and every one of us is precious in God's sight. This tender care that God has for each of God's children reminds us that we are indeed part of one family, that we are together joined across our differences by sharing equally in God's image, reflecting in our faces the diversity of God. Because of this beautiful diversity within God's family, we look beyond our immediate blood relations to see ourselves connected most fully with the whole human race. That family, though far from perfect, is held together by God. Flawed as we are, we work to show a love for one another that God first showed to us.

Questions for Reflection

1. What are the ways our society (or our church or community in particular) tries to make sense of death?
2. Who are the modern-day equivalents of Sarah and Rachel? And how does this story help us empathize with and understand today's Sarahs and Rachels better?
3. In what ways do the stories about death in the Bible illuminate deaths in our own communities and families?
4. How can we, as the people of God, side with those who are killed unjustly?
5. How have you been influenced by the death of someone in your family, both narrowly and widely construed? What was your grieving process like?

Conclusion

As you come to the end of this book, you might have more questions than answers. More confusion than clarity. Perhaps you are even more perplexed about families than when you first began. If we are describing your situation, then this book has served its function. And this function was to show you how complicated the issues and problems faced by families were and still are; and how these complications are reflected in the vibrant stories of the Hebrew Bible. These stories are not as simple and straightforward as you might have assumed or were taught, but neither have the lives of families ever been uncomplicated, whether in the stories written thousands of years ago or today. We wanted to make your conception and understanding of the family and that of the stories in the Bible richer and more multivalent.

In so doing, we have tried to use the ancient stories in the Bible as the lens through which to reflect upon and discuss a myriad of tales and topics concerning the family. We have struggled with difficult subjects such as infertility, abuse, trauma, infighting between siblings, equality in the church, and coming out as LGBTQ. Other challenging concerns, such as blended families, trailing spouses, and singleness, were also considered. Through these discussions, we have reflected on what it means to be a family and how familial issues are not just about family alone but about our relationships with God.

Threads That Bind the Book

As we have seen, relationships amongst family members can be both loving and contentious, sometimes simultaneously. The relationship between these same family members and God, and family units and God can be likewise complicated. In approaching these complications, this book has surveyed a variety of biblical episodes and relationship topics, and has found three threads or themes that unite them. The first is that families are much more expansive in definition than they first appear. Families are not just people who are related to each other by blood or by law but can consist of any group with shared ties, relationships, and affiliations. As such, our friends, fellow church members, ministers, work colleagues, fellow volunteers, or pets can be and should be deemed as part of our family. According to this expansive definition of the family, we are all a member of a family, and likely, members of multiple families. None of us are ever really alone. Never truly family-less.

Indeed, according to this wider vision of families, we can even be a part of a family which consists of a single person who is in relationship with their God. And this understanding leads to our next thread or theme that emerged from these chapters: Issues concerning the family are not simply only about the family but also involve God and are theologically significant. Family problems, in other words, affect our relationship with God in some way. If all of us are members of multiple families, including the human family, then we are beholden to them. As members of these various families, we bear responsibility for the welfare of others in the numerous families to which we belong. As our definition of the family increases, so does our sense of responsibility.

This has theological implications. If God with whom we are in relationship is also part of our various families, then this responsibility is entangled with and involves God. God is always part of our families, and as such, deeply affected by and involved in how we treat our other family members. The biblical stories—by portraying God as talking directly to Hagar or Rebekah, for example—merely make literal this fact: God is always present in the issues—the messiness—of our families. Jacob's wrestling match with a figure, who might be an angel, God, or his brother, perfectly encapsulates this idea.

This point brings us to the final running thread, which is a truism, but one that should provide a bit of comfort; and it is that being in a family is difficult, complicated, and messy. The biblical stories point to this repeatedly, never shying away from the dysfunctions and struggles involved in being a part of the family. Being a member of a family, the stories tell us, entails a long and perhaps never-ending process of learning, forgiving, and moving on. There may be moments of healing and moments of possible reconciliation but never perfection. Even when Jacob and Esau reconcile at the end, even as they weep and hug each other, we know that in the future these brothers will become two different nations, two different families, who will at points again try to thieve and hurt each other. Perfect families, the stories tell us, do not and cannot exist—not even in the Bible!—because families are made up of people who are themselves so very imperfect, so very fallible.

Goals of the Book

These three themes that we have seen in the chapters of this work—that families should be understood expansively, that families are theologically significant, and that families are complex—resonate with the three goals of the book, which we outlined in the introduction. The first goal, if you recall, is that the biblical text is a relevant reflection of and mirror for some of the pain and problems in our own world. As our brief recap of the themes indicates, it is precisely because the biblical text refuses to shy away from portraying the difficulties and complexities inherent in families—because it so brazenly airs the dirty laundry of the first families of Israel—that these stories remain so familiar and so pertinent.

This is especially the case because, as we explained in the introduction, we have tried to read the biblical stories relationally. We have let these stories speak to us and teach us; and conversely, we have, at points, spoken back to these stories, perhaps even angrily or in exasperation. We have, in other words, been in relationship with these stories, and the God who emerges from them, and in so doing, we have seen in them reflections of our own issues, questions, concerns, and fears, especially about our families.

We have also, hopefully, seen God reflected in and through these stories. These reflections of and about God most likely emerged when we paid close attention to the voices in the Scriptures that are usually silenced. The silences and quiet might have been the deliberate work of the biblical authors or the effect of wrong and misguided interpretations. As we hope we have shown in this work, hearing these dimmed voices is urgent and essential. It is only by listening to them, be they of Eve, Hagar, or Ishmael, that we can learn to hear the voice of God, which, many times, overlaps with and is channeled through these muted voices. Indeed, according to the biblical text, God's voice or presence literally consists of the sound of muted or dimmed silence (1 Kgs. 19:12). Hence, according to the Scriptures, listening to silenced voices is theologically important as it is akin to listening to the voice of God.

Moreover, listening to the silenced voices in the biblical text affects our relationship with God by affecting the relationships in our families of which God is a part. By learning to hear these muted voices, we practice and become better at hearing the dimmed voices in our various families, be they in our immediate family, or expanding outward, in our larger families like our church, our community, and our world. By learning to listen, for example, to the voice of Hagar in the text as she is wandering in the desert looking for water, we become better adept at hearing the voices of modern Hagars in our churches, communities, or even in our immediate families who might also be similarly lost and wandering in deserts. In becoming better listeners of muted or silent voices, we also become more empathetic and more able to partner with God in helping to take care of the various family members in our midst. As God, according to the Scriptures, heeded Hagar's voice, providing her with life-giving water, so we too can become more attuned to and therefore better allies of God as God works to heed the ignored or unheard voices of the modern Hagars in our families.

Building on these two goals, our last goal of this work was to help you, readers, to deepen your relationships and make more meaningful connections with your families and communities of faith. We hope that, through our relational reading of these stories, which has shown families to be expansive, theologically significant, and complex, we have convinced you of the relevance of these ancient tales and have moved you to practice empathy with characters whose voices are dimmed in the biblical narrative. In so doing, we hope that this has led to deeper conversations either internally or with others, and has provoked you to ask braver and sometimes uncomfortable questions about the text, God, and families; and we hope that through these rich conversations that your connections and relationships with each other, with God, or even just with yourself have become strengthened and refreshed.

Notes

Chapter 1: Not Good to Be Alone?

1. Phyllis Trible, "Eve and Adam: Genesis 2–3 Reread," *Andover Newton Quarterly* (March 1973): 251–58.
2. "Satan" is capitalized here because the interpretation linking the serpent and Satan assume that this is a particular figure with this particular name. This is in contrast to the use of "satan" in the Hebrew Bible where satan is not a personal name but a job title, meaning the "accuser."
3. For more on the missing phrase in Genesis 3:6, see Julie Faith Parker, "Blaming Eve Alone: Translation, Omission, and Implications of עמה in Genesis 3:6b," *Journal of Biblical Literature* 132 (2013): 729–47.
4. Albertina Saravia, *Popol Wuh: Ancient Stories of the Quiche Indians of Guatemala, Illustrated with Drawings from the Mayan Codices* (Guatemala: Editorial Piedra Sanata, 1991).
5. Saravia, *Popol Wuh*, 33.
6. Saravia, *Popol Wuh*, 42.
7. Saravia, *Popol Wuh*, 42–44.
8. Richard Davidson with Susan Begley, *The Emotional Life of Your Brain* (New York: Penguin Group, 2012), 143.

Chapter 2: Brothers' Keepers

1. James Kugel, *The Bible as It Was* (Cambridge, MA: Harvard University Press, 1997), 86–87.
2. The Masoretic Text of Genesis 4:8 has the following: "Cain said to his brother, Abel. . . . And when they were in the field, Cain rose up against his brother Abel and killed him."
3. Elie Wiesel, "Cain and Abel: 'He who kills, kills his brother,'" *Bible Review* 14, no. 1 (February 1998): 20–21.
4. "A Fractured Inheritance," *The Good Place*, season 3, episode 6, originally aired November 1, 2018. Created by Michael Schur.

Chapter 3: Trauma and Family Interventions

1. On ancient interpretations of Noah, see James L. Kugel, *The Bible as It Was* (Cambridge, MA: Harvard University Press, 1997), esp. 97–120.
2. On the various interpretations of Noah's nakedness and the interpretation of this passage, see John Sietze Bergsma and Scott Walker Hahn, "Noah's Nakedness and the Curse of Canaan (Genesis 9:20–27)," *Journal of Biblical Literature* 124 (2005): 25–40.
3. Ilona Rashkow, "Daddy-Dearest and the 'Invisible Spirit of Wine': Themes and Variations," in *Taboo or Not Taboo: Sexuality and Family in the Hebrew Bible* (Minneapolis: Fortress Press, 2000), 93–113.
4. On the subject of Ham's curse and its use in the justification of slavery, see David M. Goldenberg, *The Curse of Ham: Race and Slavery in Early Judaism, Christianity, and Islam* (Princeton: Princeton University Press, 2003); Stephen R. Haynes, *Noah's Curse: The Biblical Justification of American Slavery* (Oxford: Oxford University Press, 2002).
5. For a list of states that list clergy as mandatory reporters of child abuse, and for excerpts from state laws, see https://www.childwelfare.gov/pubPDFs/clergymandated.pdf.
6. For more on family systems theory, read Edwin Friedman, *From Generation to Generation: Family Process in Church and Synagogue* (New York, London: The Guilford Press, 1985); Peter L. Steinke, *How Your Church Family Works: Understanding Congregations as Emotional Systems* (Herndon, VA: The Alban Institute, 1993).

Chapter 4: Trailing Spouses (or Family Moves)

1. Nahum Sarna, *Genesis: The Traditional Hebrew Text with New JPS Translation*, The JPS Torah Commentary (Philadelphia: Jewish Publication Society, 1989), 88.
2. Bureau of Economic Analysis, https://www.bea.gov/data/intl-trade-investment/activities-us-multinational-enterprises-mnes.
3. Pew Research Center, https://www.pewresearch.org/fact-tank/2019/08/29/facts-about-american-workers/.

Chapter 5: Dealing with Infertility

1. Karen Propp, "Sarah's Laugh: How Infertile Women Deal," *Reproductive Health Matters* 7 (1999): 39–42.
2. RESOLVE: The National Infertility Association, https://resolve.org/support/for-friends-and-family/.

Chapter 6: Blended Families

1. Joel Kaminsky, "Humor and the Theology of Hope: Isaac as a Humorous Figure," *Interpretation* 54 (2000): 363–75.
2. Delores Williams, *Sisters in the Wilderness: The Challenge of Womanist God-Talk* (Maryknoll, NY: Orbis, 1993), 15–20.
3. Williams, *Sisters in the Wilderness*, 160–61.
4. Adeel Hassan, "Hate-Crime Violence Hits 16-Year High, F.B.I Reports," *New York Times*, November 12, 2019, https://www.nytimes.com/2019/11/12/us/hate-crimes-fbi-report.html.
5. Jennifer Eberhardt, *Biased: Uncovering the Hidden Prejudice That Shapes What We See, Think, and Do* (New York: Viking, 2019), 7.

Chapter 7: Who Will Save Isaac?

1. Elie Wiesel, *Messengers of God: Biblical Portraits and Legends* (New York: Simon & Schuster, 1976), 75.
2. Carol Delaney, *Abraham on Trial: The Social Legacy of Biblical Myth* (Princeton: Princeton University Press, 1998).
3. Wiesel, *Messengers of God*, 83.
4. Wiesel, *Messengers of God*, 97.
5. Susan Cottrell, email message to author, July 31, 2020.
6. Lindsay Schnell, "'Sometimes, Divorce Is Necessary.' Fight for LGBTQ Inclusion May Finally Split United Methodists," *USA Today*, November 22, 2019, https://www.usatoday.com/story/news/nation/2019/11/22/united-methodist-church-progressive-conservative-split-lgbtq/4233406002/.
7. Rachel Held Evans, *Searching for Sunday: Loving, Leaving, and Finding the Church* (Nashville, TN: Nelson Books, 2015).
8. Evans, *Searching for Sunday*, 34.
9. Evans, *Searching for Sunday*, 34.

Chapter 8: The Traps of Competitive Parenting

1. Emily V. Gordon, "Why Women Compete with Each Other," *New York Times*, October 31, 2015, https://www.nytimes.com/2015/11/01/opinion/sunday/why-women-compete-with-each-other.html.
2. Robert Putnam, *Our Kids: The American Dream in Crisis* (New York: Simon & Schuster, 2015).
3. Betty Hart and Todd R. Risley, *Meaningful Differences in the Everyday Experience of Young American Children* (Baltimore: Paul H. Brookes, 1995); Anne Fernald, Virginia A. Marchman, and Adriana Weisleder, "SES Differences in Language Processing Skill and Vocabulary Are Evident at 18 Months," *Developmental Science* 16 (March 2013): 234–48, quoted in Putnam, *Our Kids*, 116, n. 43.
4. Jason DeParle, *A Good Provider Is One Who Leaves: One Family and Migration in the 21st Century* (New York: Viking, 2019).

Chapter 9: Reconciling with Your Siblings as an Adult

1. This chapter consists of several stories. If you are using this for preaching or for study, you can choose to focus on one or more of these narratives.
2. Sarah Griffiths, "The Effect of Childbirth No-one Talks About," BBC Future, April 24, 2019, https://www.bbc.com/future/article/20190424-the-hidden-trauma-of-childbirth.
3. Marcel Mauss, *The Gift: Forms and Functions of Exchange in Archaic Societies*, trans. Ian Cunnison (Glencoe, IL: The Free Press, 1954).
4. Paul Ricoeur, *The Course of Recognition*, trans. David Pellauer (Cambridge: Harvard University Press, 2007).

Chapter 10: A Death in the Family

1. Joel Kaminsky, "Humor and the Theology of Hope: Isaac as a Humorous Figure," *Interpretation* 54 (2000): 363–75.
2. *The Farewell*, directed by Lulu Wang (New York: A24, 2019).

3. See the mural in the video in Joseph Hincks, "In Solidarity and as a Symbol of Global Injustices, a Syrian Artist Painted a Mural to George Floyd on a Bombed Idlib Building," *Time*, June 6, 2020, https://time.com/5849444/george-floyd-mural-idlib-syria/.
4. "Maternal Mortality," Centers for Disease Control and Prevention, https://www.cdc.gov/nchs/maternal-mortality/index.htm.
5. "Pregnancy-Related Deaths," Centers for Disease Control and Prevention, https://www.cdc.gov/reproductivehealth/maternalinfanthealth/pregnancy-relatedmortality.htm.
6. "Pregnancy Mortality Surveillance System," Centers for Disease Control and Prevention, https://www.cdc.gov/reproductivehealth/maternal-mortality/pregnancy-mortality-surveillance-system.htm#trends.
7. "Maternal Mortality," Centers for Disease Control and Prevention.
8. Austin Frakt, "What's Missing in the Effort to Stop Maternal Deaths," *New York Times*, July 13, 2020, https://www.nytimes.com/2020/07/13/upshot/maternal-deaths-policy-neglect.html.
9. Amy Roeder, "America Is Failing Its Black Mothers," *Harvard Public Health*, Winter 2019, https://www.hsph.harvard.edu/magazine/magazine_article/america-is-failing-its-black-mothers/.
10. Richard A. Oppel Jr. and Derrick Bryson Taylor, "Here's What You Need to Know about Breonna Taylor's Death," *New York Times*, August 13, 2020, https://www.nytimes.com/article/breonna-taylor-police.html.